Nora Gallagher

Things Seen and Unseen

Nora Gallagher was born in Albuquerque, New Mexico, and lives in Santa Barbara, California. She has reported for *Time* and *Life* magazines, and her articles have appeared in *The New York Times Magazine*, *Los Angeles Times Magazine*, *The Village Voice*, *Mother Jones*, and the *Utne Reader*. She has been awarded residencies at the MacDowell Colony and at Blue Mountain.

Things
Seen and Unseen

Things
Seen and Unseen

A YEAR LIVED IN FAITH

Nora Gallagher

Vintage Books

A Division of Random House, Inc.

New York

FIRST VINTAGE BOOKS EDITION, NOVEMBER 1999

Library of Congress Cataloging-in-Publication Data
Gallagher, Nora.
Things seen and unseen: a year lived in faith / Nora Gallagher. —
1st ed.
p. cm.
ISBN 0-679-45132-3
1. Gallagher, Nora.
2. Episcopalians—California—Biography.
I. Title
BX5995.G287A3   1998
283'.092—dc21   98—13501
[B]
CIP

Vintage ISBN: 0-679-77549-8

www.vintagebooks.com

Printed in the United States of America
10 9 8

Some of the names in this book have been changed.

CONTENTS

Things
Seen and Unseen

Advent

HERE I AM in an empty church. In it, between the rows of pews, on the tile floor, under the silent cross, I walk along a boundary, a place in between heaven and earth. The Celts called it thin space. Some places were thinner than others: Lindisfarne off the northeastern coast of England, where St. Aidan led his community and prospered, and Iona, off Scotland, where Columba, the warrior monk, banished from Ireland, walked the beaches marbled with white stones flecked with green. Both are islands; they meet the mainland under water. Above me, the roof's ribs curve into its spine, an inverted keel. In this church, Trinity Episcopal in Santa Barbara, we practice to be thin, to live in space, to go through the narrow door.

I am here preparing for a Eucharist in Advent, living by a calendar that runs parallel to my Day-Timer, a counterweight, one time set against another. The church calendar calls into consciousness the existence of a world uninhabited by efficiency, a world filled with the excessiveness of saints, ashes, smoke, and fire; it fills my heart with both dread and hope. It tells of journeys and mysteries, things "seen and unseen," the world of the almost known. It dreams impossibilities: a sea divided in two, five thousand fed by a loaf and two fishes, a man raised from the dead.

My daily calendar reminds me that what I experience in the

3

world of faith must be measured against what I see, what is happening around me. I live in a world with a diminished human presence caused by technology, on what Jeremy Rifkin calls "a desacralized earth," in a country where the most sentimental aspects of psychology have joined together with the most sentimental aspects of religion to create something, not surprisingly, sentimental. A world of what Dietrich Bonhoeffer called cheap grace.

I live in a world filled with evil. And my faith cannot always endure it. My husband, who is not a Christian, fiercely says to me in the midst of an argument, "In Rwanda, fifty percent of the people were Catholic." His words stop mine on my lips: if religious faith cannot stop genocide, of what use is it at all?

And thus I doubt. Doubt is to me the handmaiden to faith, its cop, the one that keeps faith straight. To doubt is an indication of freedom and a guard against fanaticism. But it is also so easy to doubt, so easy to be cynical, that the job appears to be to enlarge the part that believes, but only to enlarge it by taking the path made painful by the doubt and with the integrity born of the doubt rather than the inflation born of sentiment, heightened emotion, or the sometimes false camaraderie of a faith community.

In "The Production of the World," his essay on Van Gogh, John Berger writes: "For an animal its natural environment and habitat are a given; for a man [sic] . . . reality is not a given: it has to be continually sought out, held—I am tempted to say salvaged."

Faith is the name I put to the seeking out, the holding, the salvage operation.

TODAY IS THURSDAY, December 1, in my Day-Timer. On the church calendar, it is a feast day for Nicholas Ferrar, an English deacon who died three hundred and fifty-seven years ago, in 1637. Nicholas left a promising political career in Parliament to start a community of laypeople at his family's estate, Little Gidding, where, as the *Oxford Dictionary of the Christian Church* puts it, "they visited and relieved the poor and the sick, taught children psalms and were skilled in the art of bookbinding." Bookbinding, I think, as I set up the candlesticks for this service; what made Nicholas leave what the dictionary calls "the brilliant career opening before him" for binding books? Was it the same thing that lured me away from a career in journalism?

Advent is the beginning of the Christian New Year. It starts four Sundays before Christmas. In the Advent Gospels, John the Baptist wanders in the wilderness, the angel Gabriel visits Mary. John and Mary each hear a voice and give a reply. "Prepare the way of the Lord, make his paths straight," says John. "How can this be?" asks Mary. (God's "intimate promise," as one woman writer put it, and "Mary's appalled assent.")

In Advent the holy breaks into the daily. In a postcard of a fifteenth-century triptych I have on my desk, Mary sits in a flowing red dress near a fireplace in the center panel. Ordinary life is in evidence around her: she reads a book; a kettle hangs in a nook near two dish towels. Gabriel sits at a little round table near her, his gold wings pressed against the wall, one pale hand on his knee. His face is full of hopeful urgency, but Mary's is calm; she has to finish this chapter. In the next room, Joseph, oblivious, carves a piece of wood. In his poem about Breughel's *Icarus*, W. H. Auden writes: "when the aged are reverently, passionately waiting / For the miraculous birth, there always must be / Children who did not specially want it to happen, skating / On a pond at the edge of the wood."

I DON'T FEEL particularly ready this year. I'm not even sure what "ready" means. I set up a small pine table we rescued from the men's room for an altar, and a row of chairs. In the kitchen microwave, I defrost the communion bread (or "zap Jesus," as the sexton, Sam, puts it). In the sacristy, a little room to the left of the main altar area, I pour Christian Brothers sherry through a plastic funnel into a small pottery jug marked with a "V" for "vin." Out of a tall bureau with flat narrow drawers, I lift a folded linen cloth the size of a napkin, called a purificator, embroidered with a cross, and ironed by Martha Smith, a member of the Altar Guild. These bits and pieces of a ritual nearly two thousand years old I place in a basket and set down near the small altar.

The church is filled with domesticity renamed: dishes become patens for the bread and cups become chalices for the wine; napkins and tablecloths become purificators and corporals (a cloth placed on top of the altar at the beginning of communion to catch the corporal—the body—crumbs from the Eucharist bread); candles are torches, bread the body, wine the blood. When a friend of mine who is a priest showed off his newly furbished church to a young Japanese woman who had never seen a Christian church, she took one look at the altar and said, "Oh, you have a meal here."

Episcopalians are Anglo-Catholics, in tradition if not always in practice. That is, we are a Catholic church separated from Rome. In 1529, Henry VIII had given up his quest to have the pope pronounce his marriage annulled and turned toward convincing Parliament of the need for a new church. By 1534, England had an English church with the king as its head. We are a church born in the lust and ambition of a king, at a time that coincided with the Reformation sweeping Europe. (A time when "radical theology smuggled in from Germany happened to coincide with a political impasse between royal and papal spheres of influence," as an English priest put it.) Henry ordered all his priests to read a declaration against the pope in church (the Archbishop of York pointed out that the order would be hard to obey because many of his curates could not read). He dissolved the monasteries and confiscated their land. Some of the abbeys were demolished—one was blown up with gunpowder; others slowly fell into ruin as their stones were removed to build walls and barns. Monastery bells, altars, vestments, candlesticks, organs, roof tiles, and pulpits were auctioned or surrendered to the state, and Catholic shrines were destroyed. But Henry was not a Protestant. He refused to change the form or language of the Mass, and punished those who wanted further reform. He attended Mass three times a day when he was hunting, it is said, and sometimes five times a day when he was not.

In January of 1547, Henry died, and reform began in earnest. Lutheran principles undergirded the many changes: the Mass was said in English; the laity were invited to become active participants, rather than spectators, during the service; priests were allowed to marry. In 1549, Henry's archbishop, Thomas Cranmer, a quiet scholar who spent three-quarters of his days at study, finished the Book of Common Prayer. Cranmer was a cautious man who believed in reform but loved what was best of the old. He was a genius at liturgy: he created a service of mattins, an office of evensong, and a Mass that combined medieval rites with Protestant simplicity. It was "at once delicate and austere," as the English historian Owen Chadwick writes, "the work of a single mind." It remains one of the most beautiful guides to worship in the world. The Anglican wedding vows—"For better for worse, for richer for poorer, in sickness and in health"—are Cranmer's.

In the United States, the Episcopal Church is named for its bishops—*episcopus* means bishop in Latin—as high as our hierarchy goes. The country is divided into dioceses; each diocese is headed by a bishop. Each parish is headed by a priest—they are called priests—and an elected board of laypeople called a vestry. Episcopal priests are free to marry (since 1549) and women have been ordained to the priesthood since 1974.

In the last twenty years, the Episcopal Church has changed, beginning with the ordination of women and continuing with a revision of the Book of Common Prayer in 1979. (Cranmer's prayer book was revised twice in England and then revised in 1789 for the American church. Two more revisions followed before the current edition.) Recognition of lay ministry was one of the driving forces behind the revised prayer book: laypeople now regularly serve at the altar, read prayers, visit the sick, and even, though rarely, preach. Presently, the church is arguing over the ordination of openly gay men and lesbian women to the priesthood. (There are, of course, many homosexuals who are priests; but they are usually in awkward positions in their churches, halfway in and halfway out of the closet.) All these changes have caused trouble, sometimes near schism, but they reflect a church born in reformation and continuing to re-form.

To those outside the Church, much of this may appear irrelevant, like counting angels dancing on the tip of a pin. The Episcopal Church, like other mainstream faiths, began losing members in the 1970s. (In that decade, church membership declined 15 percent.) Generally, that loss can be traced to the baby boom generation, who dropped out of mainline churches in droves and did not return. I, who was baptized in 1965 at St. John's Cathedral in Albuquerque, New Mexico, when I was fifteen, dropped out when I was twenty. But many of those who left are returning, as I did. What we find is a church different from the one we grew up in, and oddly the same: its language has changed, its priests are more accessible (and more harassed—fewer members means less money for staff), and its members are now a mix of our parents' generation, a few people in their twenties, and us. But false piety and forced fellowship are still abundant, arguments over the placement of pews take up precious time, and the Doxology ("Praise God from whom all blessings flow") is still sung at some services. For many of us, "returnees" of the boomer generation, the Church is both familiar and a foreign planet. To cope, we are often ambivalent. I never expected to be a leader in an, uh, institution. I keep looking over my shoulder to find out if someone has guessed that I'm an impostor. I walk a sometimes amusing and sometimes scary tightrope between compromise and pushing for more change, or a better fit between me and this Church. But if the Church hadn't changed, I wouldn't be here. The first time I saw a woman celebrate at the altar fundamentally changed my relationship to Church and to God.

The service tonight is one devised by five women—two priests and three laypeople—in the hopes of having one service a week that reflected "inclusive" language, a liturgy in which the pronouns associated with the Divine are not all male.

In the gathering darkness, illuminated by the candles, men and women arrive for the service. Lois and Ben Hitz, a couple in their sixties, lean and fit, newly retired. He recently converted to the Roman Catholic Church, she is a member here, and they both come to this service. Dianne Armstrong, an English professor at the local community college; Barbara Kelly, a member of the Third Order of St. Francis, the lay arm of the Franciscan Order of Monks; Kati Smith, a fund-raiser for the local food bank; Mark Grotke, a therapist from St. Michael's Episcopal Church at the university; Rachel Kelly, the secretary at Trinity; and Mark Asman, Trinity's present priest.

We use a collect, an opening prayer, written by Janet Morley, a laywoman in England:

9

O unknown God,
whose presence is announced
not among the impressive
but in obscurity;
come, overshadow us now,
and speak to our hidden places. . . .

"Creator, Redeemer, Sanctifier," we say as we cross ourselves; "May God be with you" rather than "The Lord be with
you." The presiding priest at the service is a woman, Martha
Siegel, who entered the priesthood after a successful career in
nursing and teaching. The homily is preached by a layperson,
me. The confession is changed, from "We acknowledge and
bewail our manifold sins and wickedness, which we . . . most
grievously have committed against thy divine Majesty, provok-
ing most justly thy wrath and indignation against us," to "We
confess that we have sinned against you, resisting your will in
our lives. We have not honored you in ourselves, in each other,
and in the world you have made."

Finally, we do what people like us have been doing for
thousands of years: we hide in the darkness, in silence, and try
to pray. "Prayer is religion in act; that is, prayer is real religion,"
said Auguste Sabatier, a French theologian, in 1897.

Religion is nothing if it be not the vital act by which
the entire mind seeks to save itself by clinging to the
principle from which it draws its life. This act is prayer,
by which term I understand no vain exercise of words,
no mere representation of sacred formulae, but the very
movement itself of the soul, putting itself in a personal
relation of contact with the mysterious power of which
it feels the presence—it may be even before it has a
name by which to call it. Whenever this interior prayer
is lacking, there is no religion; wherever, on the other

hand, this prayer rises and stirs the soul, even in the absence of forms or doctrines, we have living religion.

A friend calls it "going out on a limb."

I CAME TO this church five years ago as a tourist and ended up a pilgrim. What I wanted at the time I walked in the door for the late morning Mass was peace, I told myself. I believe I understood peace at the time as comfort. What I got was "The peace of God that passes all understanding," as the prayer book says—or, as an old Irish hymn goes, "The peace of God—it is no peace."

It was the late summer; I was greeted at the door by an African-American man with a sweet, vague smile and handed a bulletin by a thin woman with a sharp unhappy face. Inside, it was dark and cool; the altar stood beneath a stained-glass window facing east, as is the pattern in many churches. Men and women sat in lonely isolation in the mostly empty pews; the priest at the time, a dark-haired middle-aged man who looked depressed, preached a sermon about codependence.

For the next few months, I dropped in on Trinity a few Sundays a month. I kept wondering why I was there but couldn't leave. The priest continued to seem depressed; the congregation dwindled: in a church that held four hundred, eighty to one hundred and twenty-five attended Mass on Sunday, five or six during the week. Very few people spoke to me at the coffee hour. Then, in the midst of this unhappy place, funny things began to happen. A couple of us started a soup kitchen in the parish hall. When the Jesuit priests and their housekeepers were killed in El Salvador in the spring of 1990, we held a candlelight vigil for them. We expected a hundred people; four hundred fifty—many from the community at large—showed up. A member of the parish wrote a letter to the bishop of the Diocese of Los Angeles complaining about the priest and, after a long process, he eventually resigned. People were waking from a long sleep. During that time, I was often frustrated, disconcerted, even disoriented, but I was also waking to myself.

"I wake to sleep, and take my waking slow . . ." wrote Theodore Roethke. "I learn by going where I have to go."

At Trinity, I learned how to speak to a crowd, how to write prayers, how to make soup for two hundred out of discarded vegetables. I cleaned up my act, stopped rebelling against everything in front of me (and/or leaving or hiding), and claimed my piece of the pie. I helped my friend Ben Nistal-Moret die—his was the first dead body I had ever seen—and I ran up against my own nature everywhere I went. "For now we see through a glass, darkly;" said St. Paul, "but then face to face."

"You were in a seeking mode," said a friend I made at Trinity, Ed Potts, a college administrator. "Now you are in a finding mode."

In the midst of it, I learned something about faith, its mucky nature, how it lies down in the mud with the pigs and the rabble. When Ben realized he was dying, he asked me to be his "alternate health care agent." As I signed that section of his living will, I imagined standing in the hallway of a hospital with perhaps a few doctors in white coats making compassionate and elegant decisions, gracefully. I did not imagine what came to pass. Instead of that antiseptic corridor, I sat in Ben's living room, jet-lagged, shoveling Chinese takeout food into my mouth, my own house strewn with dirty laundry and used cat-litter boxes. I was deciding whether or not to ask a doctor to get a new drug that would help end Ben's life. I had not imagined being so tired I wanted Ben to hurry up and die. In short, I had imagined a better version of myself. Instead I was the same old fucked-up woman.

In that time, I learned that everything is God's: my fucked-up self, my dirty laundry, my harrowing inability to be perfect for Ben. Everything is God's: shame, suicide, assisted death, AIDS. Because God is inside everything, findable in everything, because—I became convinced—I would not have made it through Ben's death without God. God is not too good to hang out with jet-lagged women with cat-litter boxes in their dining rooms, or men dying of AIDS, or, for that matter, someone nailed in humiliation to a cross. God is not too good for anything.

I learned about community: that being faithful to God means being faithful to others, in sickness and in health, for better for worse.

In my journal of July 1990, I copied down a quote from the Czech president, Václav Havel: "By perceiving ourselves as part of the river," wrote Havel, "we take responsibility for the river as a whole."

I began to understand that the Holy Spirit (who is clearly a scatterbrained woman at a very large computer in heaven) may or may not give a damn about results, but cares about the human process of getting there. Each time we met at Trinity to plan a worship service, to balance the budget, to decide how to decorate for Easter, we ran up against envy, pride, and sloth. And we felt grace, learned compassion—for ourselves and for others—and sometimes, even sensed rebirth. "Be like the fox / " writes Wendell Berry, "who makes more tracks than necessary, / some in the wrong direction. / Practice resurrection."

Once, at Mount Calvary Monastery in Santa Barbara, a house of the Order of the Holy Cross, an Anglican religious order, a young cleric sat down at a table with me and a great bishop of the church, Daniel Corrigan. Dan was in his eighties at the time, retired, still strong as an ox. For most of his life, he had defied authority for the sake of compassion. In Germany, at the end of the First World War, he fed starving German children against naval regulations and then spent time in the brig;

in 1963 he was arrested trying to integrate an amusement park near Baltimore; he said Mass on the steps of the Pentagon to protest the war in Vietnam. In the early seventies—when he was in his seventies—he advocated the ordination of openly gay priests at the Episcopal General Convention. In 1974, in Philadelphia on the feast day of Saints Mary and Martha, Dan and two other retired bishops ordained eleven women deacons to the priesthood, without benefit of church permission. He was chastised, isolated, threatened with excommunication. Two years later, the General Convention voted to ordain women.

As we were eating together, the young priest was suddenly overcome with earnestness.

"Bishop Corrigan," he asked, through a mouthful of French toast, "What would you die for?"

"Water rights," Dan replied, without missing a beat.

The boy sat back in his chair. Dan smiled. "Why not?" he asked. Then he continued, "You don't actually get up one morning and decide to die for something. You put your foot on a path and walk. One day, you look back, maybe fifty years, and say, 'That's what I gave my life for.'"

I understood that Trinity was where I was meant to muck around, to unlearn habits, to give my life. When I was asked by an Episcopal laywoman, in a guided meditation, to imagine a house and a family inside, mine had a dining table full of people from the parish.

EVERY SUNDAY AT TRINITY, we said the Lord's Prayer together. We settled into it like chickens hunkering down to roost, like people entering into the houses of their childhoods. Sometimes we became one voice, one rhythm, and I was carried on a sea of voices. "Our Father, who art in Heaven, hallowed be thy name."

When we said "hallowed" I could feel a hollow place open

up in me. As a child learning the prayer, having no idea what "hallowed" meant, I had imagined making a cave for God's name in the banks of the irrigation ditches that flowed past our house. I was not far off: to hallow, to make holy, is to make a place both inside and outside the self, a space fit for God, God-shaped.

The world of parish life has about it a "quietly invisible, mystical interconnectedness," wrote Scott Peck. As I went to church and worked in the soup kitchen and on various projects, I got to know and feel that interconnectedness, the web of relationships formed in a house where people are trying to keep their souls alive, attempting a resuscitation. The communion of saints, as Dorothy Day, the founder of the Catholic Worker, said, is the communion of workers.

In the soup kitchen, a woman stood next to me in the serving line. "I was listening to Rush Limbaugh today and he says there are towns that coddle the homeless and I couldn't help but feel that we do that here in Santa Barbara," she said. We both looked out at the tables where homeless men were eating zucchini soup that the cook had made from discarded vegetables. I said I thought it was probably pretty tough to be poor in Santa Barbara because it was so hard to get a roof over your head or to find a bathroom. Even to sit down. She hesitated, then nodded. She said, "You know I think actually my family is just about a medical bill and a tax payment away from the street. My husband was laid off in August." She went on, "We are just stuck together with Scotch tape and baling wire to look presentable."

One Sunday morning, a young man took me aside. Pulling a purple medallion out of his pocket, he said, "I wanted you to see this." On it was written, "One month sober."

Betty Bickel, a woman in her late sixties, asked me if she should run again for the vestry. "Or am I one of those old people that should be put out to pasture and doesn't know it?"

I went to see Barbara Kelly in the hospital. Cancer had metastasized to her spine; she lay in bed full of morphine and pain. Her husband, Frank, napped in a nearby chair. He had been a speechwriter for Harry Truman, then moved to Santa Barbara to work for the Center for Democratic Institutions. Barbara raised their two sons, wrote poetry, and became a member of the Third Order of St. Francis. Barbara was wholeheartedly honest. She said her pain "obliterated my sense of humor, my confidence, my joy in other people, even my easiness in prayer.

"Through it all I have held on to one message—'I will be with you,' " she said. "But I reply, 'Where are you exactly, Lord?' "

Four of us went to see Wim Wenders's movie *Faraway, So Close!,* about an angel who decides to become a man. Over coffee after the movie, David Griffin, a professor at the School of Theology at Claremont, said, "He had such a hard time. Even though he had lived forever, he wasn't prepared to be human."

Added Ann Jaqua, a spiritual director, "I don't know that anything prepares us to be human."

THESE WERE THE HALLOWED PLACES. In the soup kitchen, Robert Hagler, the prior of Mount Calvary Monastery, dressed in his white robe, sang, "I can't help it if I'm still in love with you," while stirring a pot of chili. One morning when Ben was still alive, he and I and a mild man in the early stages of senility worked in the kitchen. Ben was defrosting string beans. The gentleman, standing near the freezer, carefully took each package of beans that Ben removed from the freezer, and put it back in. "Before I figured out what was going on," Ben said, "I thought it was some kind of reverse miracle."

As he grew sicker and could no longer eat, Ben managed to pour more of himself into narrower and narrower spaces. An architectural conservator, he had restored a Roman cloister in Arles and Civil War monuments in the South, written on Mexican art museums, taught medieval restoration, and swung the incense thurible at New York City's St. John the Divine. (He swung it "erotically," a friend from New York said after his death.) Now, fed intravenously from a bag of nutrients he carried in a backpack, he made meatloaf in the soup kitchen, the best meatloaf I'd ever tasted, with a sauce of sharp, tangy flavors and a moist inner heart. I asked him how he could stand to cook when he couldn't eat, and he replied, "I taste the smells." He smoked chickens in the smoker his lover, Mark Grotke, gave him for Christmas, consulted with the Mission of San Gabriel on their southern wall, made a high tea for five. In between, he threw up, sweated out fevers, fainted from diarrhea, and had tubes pushed down his throat, into his liver, and up his intestines. His feet and belly swelled and the whites of his eyes turned the color of lemons. He made hotels for my cats out of the boxes the pharmacy used to deliver his liquid diet bags and reported to me while I was staying in France which cat slept where. Two weeks before he died, he preserved olives he had picked at Mount Calvary Monastery, driving up every twenty-four hours to stir them in brine—with a wooden spoon, he noted, not a metal one.

The metaphor he choose for his life near its end was exact. "I feel as if all of my life were being pushed through a small opening. It's all coming down to this," he said, bringing his hands together to form a funnel.

ONE MORNING, I walked out of the kitchen into the dining room and found a long line of men where no one had been five minutes before.

"Where did you guys come from?" I asked in astonishment.

"You're so good-looking, honey," replied a tall fellow with tattoos all over his arms. "You're drawing a crowd."

Priests kiss the stole, the long strip of cloth worn over vestments, before placing it around their necks. Back in the dishwasher room, Ann Jaqua paused when putting on her apron and kissed the neck string. Priest of the Soup Pot. The Holy Spirit as an Italian cook.

Esther de Waal, an English historian who has written extensively about Celtic Christianity, writes, "It was a practice in which ordinary people in their daily lives took the tasks that lay to hand but treated them sacramentally, as pointing to a greater reality which lay beyond them. It is an approach to life which we have been in danger of losing, this sense of allowing the extraordinary to break in on the ordinary."

BY THE END of the Advent service, deep pools of dark fill the church, the candlelight is thin. So much of Advent is centered in the play between the dark of winter and the frail light of candles. We end the service with a blessing:

> *The blessing of God,*
> *who has promised*
> *to come into our lives,*
> *be with you today.*
>
> *The blessing of God,*
> *whose love ransoms us*
> *from all captivity,*
> *be with you forever.*
>
> *The blessing of God,*
> *whose breath brings new beginnings,*

send you forth into the world
to create a new day for the good of all. Amen.

Then we blow out the candles and lock the front door. In the parish hall, in a circle of folding chairs, the choir is practicing for Christmas. Grey Brothers, the choirmaster, a young man with brown wavy hair and a solemn face, warms them up by having them sing "Gloria, gloria, gloria, in excelsis Deo." Grey also works at Westmont, a local Christian college, teaching music. His wife, Carrie, five months pregnant with their third child, plays the piano.

The Thursday night "base community" is meeting in the library. Modeled after the Latin American *comunidades de base*, Trinity's communities work from the same premise as do those in Latin America—that the Gospel is a living document, speaking to us aloud, shaking us up. There are two communities at Trinity, each one having ten to twelve members. Each week, we "check in" by talking about how our prayers have gone that week, then read the Gospel for the following Sunday. Then we ask ourselves, What is this saying to us in our lives right now? What is it asking us to do? In many ways, the soup kitchen came out of this scrutiny. We had read Matthew's Gospel, "When I was hungry, you fed me," enough times and talked about it so much that it became impossible not to act one day when the vestry struggled to decide what to do with so many homeless people coming to the office window begging for food.

"I could go down the street and find out if Vons would give us their old vegetables for soup," Ann Jaqua said one night at the base community.

The first year of the kitchen at Trinity, we talked about it in the base community all the time. It was as if we were inside the Gospels in a new way.

I remember one evening that year when Chris, the woman

who was hosting the community, started to talk. She had a large wooden swan dressed in what looked like a tulle ballet dress sitting above her breakfront. I had contempt for her decorating taste and for her. For most of the nine months I had known her, she had seemed to me to be a relentless Pollyanna.

Chris started speaking slowly about Ephraim, a guy who volunteered in the kitchen. I, too, knew Ephraim. He and I were doing dishes together once when I asked him, "Were you around last year, in Santa Barbara?"

"Last year," he said, "I was in jail for dealing cocaine."

One night, at Chris's invitation, he came to the base community. We were talking about Jesus and how he lived among people who were "loving and grieving." Ephraim broke in: "And hoping." Chris had really gone the mile with Ephraim. I had worried about how much time she was spending with him; I wasn't sure she knew what she was getting into. She was naive, I said to myself, a lost middle-aged woman, bent on seeing the bright side.

"I tried everything with him," she said that evening at her house. "I tried to get him hooked up with halfway houses and quit-drinking programs and drug programs and he wasn't interested. Finally I asked him, Why? He said he'd been through all of them and they were all institutions and all he wanted was a place of his own." She stopped, a wide smile on her face. I was interested.

"Now he has a little shed he lives in. It's the kind of place that was, in the places I used to live in, a shed for a lawn mower." (I heard "in the places I used to live in.") "He said he can stand up and stretch his arms out straight and not touch the walls.

"And I know that he might end up back in jail, but for now he's doing fine. I think that what we have to do in the kitchen is listen to what they have to tell us, rather than coming up with solutions on our own."

I'm an idiot, I thought. This woman has a mind. Not only does she have a mind, she's walked her way right through a whole piece of life and come out the other side with a new point of view. She's put herself out of her normal, safe milieu, lived dangerously, and discovered a new truth. I felt my harsh contempt for her melt.

Tonight, Mark Benson, a physician assistant who cares for men with AIDS in Los Angeles and who volunteers in the soup kitchen, says that for his prayers he's been reading, memorizing, and repeating poems by George Herbert, an English priest who died in 1633. "And I'm thinking of putting in a rose garden," he adds.

Mark has recently moved here from Los Angeles, where he was a member of All Saints Episcopal Church in Pasadena. All Saints is a hugely successful church, with more than eighteen hundred members and a strong commitment to social justice. At All Saints, in 1992, Mark and his partner, Philip Straw, were wed by the rector, George Regas, in what was the church's first "same-sex covenant."

Philip Straw died of AIDS later that year. In the video of their covenant one can see that he is already seriously ill. To Mark, Philip left a surprise legacy that allowed him to buy a house in Santa Barbara. The house has a view of the ocean and a lovely open deck, but it is filled with Philip's presence and therefore his absence. Philip was a musician. Mark attends the spare early service at Trinity so that he won't hear music or have to sing.

Elizabeth Reifel, a tall woman with a cloud of blond-gray hair, owns a store downtown that's a fantasy of perfect taste: Limoges enameled boxes, white china rabbits, French linens, and old jewelry. Kindness flows in her like a river, combined with an ironic, sharp mind. She peers over her faux-tortoiseshell reading glasses through watery, elusive eyes and tells us of an exchange with the director of the local museum. The museum owns the building her store is in and has just given her notice. "I pasted a smile on my face and thought evil thoughts."

Nancee Cline, a dancer, a Montessori teacher who taught her twin boys at home and is studying for her master's in literature, says she's found herself singing hymns.

Dodie Little, raised in North Carolina, ran her family's cotton mill with her brother in Wadesboro, and then decided to spend a contemplative month at Holy Savior Priory, a retreat house of the Order of the Holy Cross, in South Carolina. She stayed almost two years. Now she has moved here, to start a new life closer to the brothers of Mount Calvary.

Lois Hitz, fresh from the service, says she's glad to be out of the hospital. She's an environmentalist who was designing a show for the Museum of Science and Technology in Los Angeles when she discovered she had ovarian cancer. She was fifty-six. Since that time, she has undergone chemotherapy as well as more experimental treatments. For almost five years, the cancer was in remission but this fall it returned.

Ann Jaqua says she is waiting. "I'm not sure what for." Ann is a retreat leader and spiritual director, with forty years' experience in the Episcopal Church. A Roman Catholic friend of hers says that in another age she would have been an abbess. Ann had three daughters within four years in her twenties, raised them in Santa Barbara, then moved to Virginia when her first husband, a NASA engineer, was relocated. She had a large suburban house with a swimming pool, threw formal dinner parties, and nearly went crazy with three daughters in adolescence all at once.

One day, Ann drove her Mercedes into downtown Washington, D.C., and went to work with the Sojourners Community, a Baptist-based community committed to working with the poor and living among them, very much like the Catholic Worker. At the Sojourners she was working in the shelter one night when she happened to catch a glimpse of a homeless woman unpacking her few belongings next to her cot.

"She was lifting a few things out of a plastic bag, folding them, and placing them beside her bed. I saw, in her motions, exactly the same motions I used to fold laundry in my suburban house. I understood, suddenly, that there was no fundamental difference between us."

I tell them about my brother. In early November, Kit was diagnosed with bladder cancer. He is fifty-one. They decided to remove his bladder right after Thanksgiving. I spent that week in the hospital with him, in Albuquerque where we grew up. When he was awake we talked about our family: our loving, stubborn parents; the grandmother who may or may not have committed suicide; Kit's elder son, a gifted musician; and his younger son who had just left the Navy and found a new job near Kit's town of Polvadera. We compared notes on our experience. He, older than I, remembers more. I realized he was my childhood's historian: the one person alive who helps me know that what I experienced actually happened.

In between visits with Kit, I scanned the corridors for life. A Hispanic family sat in the corner of a small waiting room. One of the women told me her brother had gone into an unexplained coma. They waited patiently, every day, for word of a change. Once they saw me carrying a prayer book. The woman gestured to me and I sat down. She pointed to my prayer book and said, "We have this in common."

Kit flirted with the female nurses, asked them where they were born, how their dogs were doing. He made friends with the male nurses. "That Anthony," he said. "He knows just how to arrange my tubes."

His doctor arrived on the second day, in the afternoon.

"They faxed me the pathology report. It looks good, except

for one thing. They found microscopic cells in one of the lymph nodes they took out. Just one," Dr. Ortolano said.

"What does that mean?" Kit asked.

"It means that they found microscopic cells in one lymph node. It could mean they got all of them when they took that node out, or it could mean that there are more. The medical oncologist, Dr. Guidise, is coming to talk to you about chemotherapy."

"Oh, God," said my brother. "I have a tube up my nose and he wants to talk to me about chemotherapy."

When I returned home, I set in front of me a photograph of him—he's hunched over his surveyor's instrument on a hillside in New Mexico—as if I could keep him alive by holding him in my line of vision. When he sent me a letter, I stroked his name and realized our signatures were almost identical.

I placed Kit's name on the Prayer List at Trinity. Within a few days, Virginia Morgan called to ask me whether his problem was "spiritual or physical." I told her physical, and then wondered how that would change her prayers.

I made calls to friends. Cynthia said, "It's like the Holy Spirit has you in a batting cage."

Anne Howard, a local priest who works in Los Angeles as the canon to the ordinary, the assistant to the bishop, returned my call from a phone booth at the Episcopal Divinity School in Cambridge. "Yeah," she said, "and it's too bad you don't have a bat."

As I tell my story tonight at the base community, Lois Hitz looks at me with detachment. "This is the worst time," she says. "At the beginning." Later she says, "One more thing: there will always be someone who inspires hope."

"Prepare the way of the Lord, make his paths straight," cries John in the Gospel. Tonight, I see all our paths converging. Lois with cancer; me with Kit; Mark having lost his Philip;

Nancee, Ann, Dodie, Elizabeth. Here we are together, in thin space, learning how to breathe.

WHEN THE BASE COMMUNITY says compline, the last evening prayer service, at nine, the light is still on in the rector's office. Last year in July, the rector who was here when I first arrived at Trinity resigned. Mark Asman arrived in January this year, having been hired as an "interim priest" with a three-year contract, to pull the parish together. This August, however, he was offered an unusual option, experimental in this diocese: if the vestry, Mark, and the bishop agree, after twelve months Mark may be "called" as rector of Trinity, a tenured position. We are five months into this new arrangement.

Mark is forty-four, a tall balding man with an open face and a hearty laugh. He wears a black suit, clerical shirt, and collar all the time, brushes his shoulders routinely for dandruff, pops breath mints. His black oxford shoes are polished to a mirror gloss; his nails and ears are perfectly clean. He was educated at The General Theological Seminary in New York City, a beautiful oasis in Chelsea of redbrick buildings enclosing lawns and flower gardens. He was ordained in 1975, at twenty-four. When he was thirty-three, he left the small church in northern California where he was rector, moved in with his father, and went to work at I. Magnin, the clothing store, in San Francisco—"selling ties," as he puts it. Because of his intelligence and ability to lead, he rose in the ranks at I. Magnin, where he stayed for ten years. In each city where he worked, in Chicago and Los Angeles, he volunteered as a priest in a local parish. His last church was in Hollywood.

What is a priest? I asked a friend of mine, who was canon to the ordinary in a diocese on the East Coast.

"A person who is too fucked up to do anything else," he replied.

"A priest is essentially an inhabitant of the limines, or the threshold between the structure and the antistructure," wrote Urban Holmes, an Episcopal priest. "A priest is someone who has died to the world's notion of controlled success."

When Mark had been at Trinity a few weeks, a group of us had dinner with him, and I asked him how he was doing. He replied, "I'm so scared of the unknown I just jump in and try to do everything and know everything and at some point I hope I'll calm down."

Tonight, as a few of us walk with him to his car, he says he has lost one of the vestry because, as she put it, she did not agree "with Trinity's interpretation of homosexuality."

As he gets in his car, a gray-blue Saab convertible, he adds that he's waking at four every morning with the church on his mind.

"I've just remembered the other reason I left full-time ministry," he says. "It was the anxiety."

WE DO NOT KNOW how to summon him, except by hope. In the midst of the Christmas rush—shopping, wrapping presents, sending cards—Advent breaks in on me. I hear the voice of John.

At the soup kitchen just before Christmas we serve a meal of turkey, cornbread stuffing, gravy, green beans, and home-made cranberry sauce. I come in late, to serve at the salad table. A man walks across the room toward me and tries to take a salad from the trays. "If you want to, you can sit down," I say. "We'll serve you."

"You'll serve me?"

"Yes."

"A sit-down meal," he says, shaking his head in disbelief. "A sit-down meal."

I scoop out salad onto plates and the servers take them away.

It has a nice routine to it; I can see the whole room. Almost all the tables are filled with men, but near me is a table of Spanish-speaking women and children. I scoop the salad, put it on a plate, put the plate on a tray. At one point, I turn from the salad to face the room. It happens without warning, just as I turn. I see the people in the room in slow motion, as if they are moving through molasses. Their faces are shining. A middle-aged woman walks across the room holding in front of her a plate piled with food; she smiles at the man she is about to serve. Between them, for a second, I see a cord drawn taut, a connection of light. Her face is lit up. She places the food in front of him, sways slightly, as if she were on board a ship, then rights herself and walks away. One of the women with the children looks up. Our eyes meet. She points at her daughter, who is eating a huge plate of turkey and stuffing, and we both laugh.

We prepare by this, by falling down before each other. "What a waste it is to be surrounded by heaven, by a sky 'made white by angels' wings' and to be unaware of it," writes Esther de Waal. "Perhaps the first step is that we really should want to unearth God in our midst . . . [to] let the mundane become the edge of glory, and find the extraordinary in the ordinary." To find not perfection, but possibility.

Christmas

IN THE LAST DAYS of Advent we live in longing. Our food is expectation. John cries in the wilderness. "One who is more powerful than I is coming after me."

I think of John wandering among piñon trees and boulders, images of wilderness I carry, shaped when I was ten. A friend of my mother's took four children on a pack trip, on horseback, into the Brazos Wilderness in northern New Mexico with a guide from the Taos Pueblo. We rode through tiny mountain villages, and then into forests where there were no houses. We had no maps. Sometimes the aspen trees grew so thickly together we had to put our feet up on our saddle horns. At night, the stars in the sky seemed as close as my hands. Frank, our guide, who smelled of saddle soap and whiskey, sang to them in Tewa.

As we rode farther and farther into the wilderness, golden eagles wheeled above us. The yellow tip of a cougar's tail flicked once before disappearing from a ledge over my head. Rainbow trout flashed in a narrow, deep stream. I didn't know what to call it, but I felt them in me, pointing to something beyond and behind them, what a friend later called "a blazing reality." In my thirties, when I visited Wyoming and saw moose, bald eagles, a black bear, I had a clearer idea of my size as a human being, a greater sense of scale. The world is God's body, says Grace Jantzen, a theologian at the University of

Manchester in England. John cries in the wilderness, in Advent, feeling his way into God.

In the Community Kitchen we travel in a wilderness, without maps. We don't screen anyone. We have only one rule: if you are obnoxious you have to go outside. We feed people with mental illness, prostitutes, the working poor, alcoholics, homeless teenagers, drug dealers. Everyone is welcome.

There was a child in the line yesterday, a little girl who had the wise, burdened eyes of a daughter who takes care of her mother. Her mother was wearing a scarf knotted around her head and earrings like a Gypsy. She was crazy, and talked to me about the importance of love, as she sifted through the storage area for food to take home. "The Bible speaks to us of love," she said. The child tugged at her sleeve and pointed out sweet potatoes.

Old Bill came in later, in much better shape than he's been in, thinner, a white stubble on his chin, a camel coat. He looked Dickensian, like Dorrit in the poorhouse. He asked me where our manager was and I told him, as if speaking to a child, that she was on vacation. "On vacation!" he said. "With her boyfriend!" I resigned myself to another nonsense conversation when someone mentioned birds. "Wild canaries," Bill chimed in, his face full of life. "When I was a boy, there were wild canaries overhead. You could hear them, they were beautiful."

"Where was that?" I asked.

"In Rhode Island," he replied. "Where I grew up."

A MAN DROPPED his tray in front of Juli, our Monday manager, and when she went to help him pick it up, he said, "I think it's time to call the police."

"Are you asking me to call the police?" Juli said.

"Yes," he replied.

IN THE KITCHEN wilderness, the one who is coming into the world has more immediacy. We are nearer to the brink. In these last days of Advent, we await what will bind together the helpless and the powerful, what will find their meaning. We await coherence.

AT THE EUCHARIST on the third Sunday in Advent, Martha Siegel and Mark Asman serve the bread. Chris Boesch and I follow behind with the chalices. The priests' robes make a soft swishing sound ahead of me. Each person takes a sip of wine, then leaves a smudge of lips or lipstick on the cup's silver rim. I wipe it off with a purificator, turn the cup, and serve the next person. Normally, I like the rhythm of serving, cleaning, and turning (the motion is like that of a bartender polishing a glass), but today I'm absorbed by those traces of lips. I find them hard to erase. When everyone is finished, Chris and I carry the chalices into the sacristy and finish off the sacramental wine. Through the sacristy door, we hear Mark begin the final Prayer of Thanksgiving: "Eternal God, Heavenly Father, you have graciously accepted us . . ." Chris and I join hands and recite the prayer out loud: "Send us now into the world in peace and grant us strength and courage to love and serve you, with gladness and singleness of heart. . . ." In the midst of the prayer, I remember an article about Mary Leakey and the footprint of an ape she found in Africa preserved in a stretch of mud. From the imprint of the heel, Leakey concluded the ape had walked upright: she was Lucy, the first human ancestor. Each smudge on the cup, each trace of lips, is like that mark in the mud, I realize, a distinctive human print that remains, or stubbornly wishes to remain, on the eternal, after it has been drunk and passed on.

At Christmas God is clothed in human flesh. That is mystery enough, but I am wondering today if something more happens. Like the moment in mitosis, just before a cell divides completely, when DNA streams back and forth along a narrow, fragile passage, what if Christmas is a dual opening, a sudden exchange? What if our human heels mark that eternal life, mix with its mud? Then Incarnation goes both ways: God not only enters into us, we enter into God. Neither of us will ever be the same.

I BEGAN SERVING communion in the winter three years ago. After thinking and praying about it for a few months, I made an appointment with the priest who was then at Trinity. (Lay eucharistic ministers are licensed by the bishop to serve communion and must be approved by their parish priests.) He told me he would soon teach a class for LEMs, as they are unfortunately dubbed (my husband, Vincent, calls us Lunar Modules). Several of us met together on two Saturday mornings, studied handouts, and learned how to grip the chalice. What we learned bore no resemblance to what serving communion is actually like.

The first time I served, my knees and my hands shook and the words I said as I served came out a question: "The Cup of Salvation?" Until we included simple instructions in the Sunday service bulletins at Trinity—"Please guide the chalice to your lips and tip it until you have received"—many people refused to touch the chalice, leaving it to the lay minister to tilt it properly and to decide when someone's lips had actually met the wine. I lived in dread of spilling. One day, shortly after Mark Asman had arrived at Trinity, a young man in a nice tan T-shirt knelt in front of me, refused to touch the chalice, and I poured the blood of Christ all over him. His horror was matched only by mine. We stared at each other for a second or two and then I had to move on. In the sacristy afterward I whispered to Mark, "I spilled wine all over this guy." He paused while wiping off a paten, looked thoughtful, and replied, "That's too bad. I guess we'll have to burn him."

As I served Sunday after Sunday, my knees stopped shaking, but I often felt as if I were in the middle of a collision between the divine and the human. As I grew more used to it, I was less in the way. Like air or water, I was the medium through which light passed. The sensation felt instinctual, as if I were recollecting a genetic memory.

I grew to love the sacristy, its quiet, its closets of priests' stoles and white robes, the little sink for washing the chalices, the square patch of new carpet covering the hole where someone had dropped burning incense, the stone basin with the drain that leads directly into the ground so consecrated wine will not enter a sewer. The chalices are all made of silver, some simple and others ornate with cherubs and shields, climbing vines and wildflowers.

Dan Corrigan used to call the Eucharist "celebrating the mysteries." He talked about traveling to the Lakota Sioux reservation in Wisconsin in the twenties to celebrate on a Sunday.

"I traveled by horseback, it was so remote," he said. "And on the final leg, I had to cross a river. I always looked forward to crossing that river, it was like crossing from one life into another. I was not only traveling from one culture into another, leaving the world of white men and women and going into another place, but also I was traveling into the mysteries. I was going to do something there at that altar that I did not fully understand."

In Wisconsin Dan was serving communion outside once when a flock of geese wobbled over. Dan walked down the line of communicants and then got to the geese. "The Body of Christ," he said, handing each goose a piece of bread.

By the time Jesus came into the world, the ritual of sacrifice was old. And the notion that a human might be sacrificed, while rare and horrifying, had been mentioned in the Torah, in the story of Abraham and Isaac. To Jews, however, the idea of a real human sacrifice was repellent, that one would then eat the remains of such a sacrifice, beyond comprehension. In John's Gospel, Jesus says, "I am the bread of life. Eat my flesh, drink my blood." The scribes and the Pharisees in one translation reply, "This is a saying that is offensive, disgusting, and one that we can't stomach."

The Protestants who parted from Rome during the Reformation differed in their attitudes toward and interpretation of the Eucharist. The newly formed Church of England found the Eucharist central not only to worship but to faith. English reformers changed the celebration of the Eucharist from a once-a-year event for the laity (as was common in the medieval Roman Catholic Church) to a weekly communion of the people. The Sacraments are not meant to be "gazed upon or to be carried about," wrote the reformers, but "that we should duly use them." They disposed of belief in transubstantiation— that the bread and wine changed under the priest's consecration to the actual body and blood of Christ—by stating flatly that it was "repugnant to the plain words of Scripture" and that the manner in which Christ's presence was in the bread and wine was best left to God.

The Eucharist was once celebrated by priests in Latin with their backs to the people. (What John Moorman, a bishop in Britain and author of *The Anglican Spiritual Tradition*, refers to as "the blessed mutter of the Mass.") Now that the priest faces the people it's all the more mysterious, as G. K. Chesterton said, because it's so visible.

The wafers are more substantial these days, a thicker form of fish food, reflecting a theological decision by the Church that Jesus did not say, "Gum me." Trinity gets hers from the (Roman Catholic) Benedictine Sisters of Perpetual Adoration in Clyde, Missouri. They make them in two varieties, whole wheat and white, and ship them in plastic bags.

In a recent week so many things happened that made no sense I practically crawled to church. My mother and I, having enjoyed a long phase of mutual peace, fell into an old fight and wounded each other all over again; an old friend's healthy four-year-old daughter grew sick, went to the hospital, and died of leukemia; two friends Vincent and I relied on for "couple" companionship separated. I took all this to the Eucharist and sank into its depths, into its heart, into the body and the blood. I put my pain into the flesh of something, rather than into the air, into the blood of a body, into a heart. To sink in there for comfort, as only a body can give comfort, to sink my pain in deep.

Returning from communion that Sunday, I curled my tongue against the roof of my mouth and found a bit of wafer left there. I chewed it. The wine still warmed my throat and stomach. I felt a sudden sure sense of having been fed. It's food, I thought, not a metaphor for food. As I knew it to be food, so I knew my hunger for it.

The mysterious and irrational Eucharist was the only thing that day that fed my mysterious and irrational life. I asked Andrew Colquhoun, a dry-witted Scot, why he had converted from the Presbyterian Church (where he was a minister) to the Episcopal Church, where he is now a priest and brother with the Order of the Holy Cross. He replied, "I was a chaplain, working in a hospital. People were dying, being born and suffering all over the place. My theology couldn't explain the chaos. I needed the Sacrament."

THE TWO SACRAMENTS in the Episcopal Church, the Eucharist and baptism, are concrete—"things seen"—bread, wine, and water. ("We are people of water and the table," said the Superior of the Order of the Holy Cross.) Under the priest's palms, they become signs. The priest's consecration is like desire, it calls out, pulls from these ordinary elements their essential beauty, their life-giving core.

This is what I grew to see at the altar rail. We kneel at Trinity (in some churches they stand for communion) on a row of faded needlepoint cushions, stitched in another era. When I served I looked down on the haloes of balding men, strands of white showing through dye, the fallen-down help-lessness in people's eyes. But I also saw in them, just as I moved forward to serve, bits of hidden life, something about to emerge, like the look of a child just before she makes her first dive. Serving the chalice once to an elderly woman at Trinity, a retired master gardener, I saw over her head a crown of green leaves. They, too, were in the midst of something being called out of them and of hearing a voice that would lead them along right pathways and stretch into time. It is not only Jesus who is transubstantiated here, but us.

In my thesaurus one of the synonyms for "Eucharist" is "windfall."

WHEN I WALK into the Kitchen on the Thursday before Christmas, the vibes are wrong. Sometimes this space is like the best cathedral, full of quiet and peacefulness, but today the air is thick with cross-purposes. Ann Jaqua, the morning man-ager, is in a hurry to leave. I put on an apron, introduce myself to the women on the serving line, get a replacement for the dessert server, say hello to Faustino, our cook for the day, and step into the open dining room. Mark Asman is standing in line in his black suit and collar, waiting for a bowl of soup. His face is pale; this morning he gave a woman at a convalescent home last rites. Greg, a brilliant homeless man who loves to tell jokes and attend theater, is washing the dishes. I saw him last night at a play out at the university.

"Didn't I see you at *Twelfth Night?*" I ask him.

"Yeah, were you there?" He smiles. "I was in the back row."

We've hired a new janitor, Mike, a bearded, potbellied guy who takes fatherly pride in his work. He's currently dating a young woman who used to wear only Army fatigues, but now wears T-shirts and flowered jumpers. They sleep nestled in bedrolls on Trinity's stone porch.

Today, a new woman is washing down trays, Theresa, who has a Walkman plugged into her ears and is dancing, her large breasts jiggling in time. Larry, a thin dark man who always wears a green parka, works beside her at the trays, his eyes fixed on the soapy water in front of him.

I'm just settling in to work when Ephraim runs up to me and tells me a man outside on the lawn believes he's having a heart attack. I run to the lawn, where a man with a big nose wearing a rugby shirt and jeans is lying on the grass pounding his chest with one rough, scorched hand. His eyes are glistening. I kneel down beside him and grab his other hand.

"It's my heart, Nora," he says, reading my name tag. "My name's David." He shakes my hand.

"Do you want me to call an ambulance?"

"Yeah, I want the ambulance."

I rush inside, find a phone, dial 911. In a few minutes, not only an ambulance, but a fully rigged fire truck and another, smaller truck arrive. The medics climb out of the ambulance slowly, pulling on plastic gloves. They walk over and kneel down next to David.

"Do you have a history of heart trouble?" one of them asks, while he puts a blood pressure band on David's upper arm.

"Just relax," says the other.

Three firemen walk across the lawn. They talk to the medics.

"I think we picked him up yesterday," says one.

David pounds his chest. "It's my heart," he says.

"Okay, okay, just relax."

They carry a gurney over, through the flower beds, past the statue of St. Francis.

"Can you get up on it or would you like us to lift you?"

"I can get up on it."

David's getting increasingly nervous and belligerent, and the medics are increasingly rough and insensitive, but when they strap him down, everyone grows calmer.

"Are you taking me to jail?" David asks.

"Would Fred Flintstone lie to you?" one of the medics says, his gentleness bought at the price of condescension. "No, we're taking you to Cottage Hospital."

They put him in the ambulance; the fire trucks drive off, and I walk back inside.

The serving women are standing in a line with their mouths open. In front of them, towering over the table, is a guy about six feet four with a handsome, craggy face.

"I'm God," he says, flapping both arms. "I'm not taking any drugs. I smoked some marijuana last night. I drank a beer."

"Would you like some watermelon?" I ask, edging aside one of the paralyzed women. "How about a piece of bread?"

"Thanks," he says, takes the food, and goes to sit down.

A big guy comes up to me.

"Is Theresa here?"

I look around. No Theresa, no breasts.

"She was here, but I don't see her now."

He follows my glance and returns to my face. He doesn't believe me. He walks away and stands, big and slightly menacing, near the stage. A fantasy wafts through my head: he's her ex-husband and he's been trailing her; now he's going to beat her up. Right here in my kitchen.

I say a small prayer and walk toward the church office.

Greg is standing just outside the dishwasher room, a towel wrapped around his waist.

"Some are born great. Some become great," he calls out. Together he and I shout across the room, "And some have greatness thrust upon them."

THAT NIGHT AT the base community, we are just beginning to read the Gospel when two young women sneak in the door. They are both lovely, but something is not quite right; they seem fragile and exposed, like birds. One is bone thin, with long dark hair falling in a stream down her back and a face scarred with acne. The other hides sable-brown eyes behind thick glasses. Elizabeth Reifel makes a place for them beside her, and they introduce themselves: Robin and Katrina, roommates. They've been looking for a "Bible study." Dodie Little and I exchange a coded glance. They could be . . . fundamentalists.

Mark Benson reads Luke 1:39–56, the Gospel for the fourth, and last, Sunday in Advent. Mary, expectant, travels to her cousin Elizabeth's house. "Blessed are you among women," Elizabeth says, "and blessed is the fruit of your womb." Then she asks, "Why has the mother of my Lord come to me?"

Mary replies, "My soul magnifies the Lord, and my spirit rejoices in God my Savior for he has looked with favor on the lowliness of his servant." In this speech, called the Magnificat, Mary tells of a world she has glimpsed that has yet to come into being, a place where the proud are scattered, where the lowly are lifted up and the powerful are brought low, a world where the hungry are fed at last and the rich must experience what it is to be empty.

It reminds me of Martin Luther King's "I Have a Dream."

In commentaries about Mary, what is usually emphasized is her obedience. Not her courage, her passion, or her love. Not her revolutionary vocabulary. Not the lessons she taught her son.

I imagine Mary singing a song like the Magnificat to Jesus when he was a little boy. As Mary told Jesus about her dream of a new, just world, he listened to her. And he became that kingdom, in his flesh and in his blood.

This evening we talk about the year. Where have we seen the kingdom?

Ann Jaqua says she's seen the kingdom in Mark Asman and the way "he's given us his heart."

I think of a day at the soup kitchen when a man sat down at the piano and played the Moonlight Sonata.

"One morning, walking in the canyon," says Mark Benson, "a little girl showed me a leaf."

"Today a woman folded her umbrella while it rained and let herself get drenched," says one of the angels in the movie *Wings of Desire*. "At the Zoo Bahnhof, instead of saying the station's name, the conductor suddenly shouted, 'Tierra del Fuego!' "

We check in. Elizabeth Reifel notes that her ex-husband has been in town, building shelves in her new store.

"He goes to a little church in the town he lives in now," she says. "And I noticed that he was quite grumpy about his spiritual life. I said something to him about it, and he said, 'It's true, and I'm hoping you can fix it. After all, twenty years ago, you got me to be a Democrat.' "

Then it's Katrina's turn. Her voice is pinched. She says she graduated from Westmont, the Christian college, and is presently looking for a job. She hesitates, then goes on:

"When I was in college I went to a church where I was taught that homosexuality was a sin and that I should help gays convert to heterosexuality. But in my senior year I went to San

Francisco to do a semester of study for college credit. I ended up at San Francisco General Hospital as a chaplain for Sojourn Episcopal Chaplaincy. On one of my first days there, I had lunch with a member of the program who was about to be ordained an Episcopal priest. He asked me what my experience was of homosexuality. I said, 'I took a class back at school called 'Sociology of Deviant Behavior.' He said, 'Katrina, I am a gay man and that is oppressive to gays.' I felt overwhelmed and scared.

"I grew to care about several gay men at the hospital, and Jesus calls us to love every person, so I started to challenge my own opinions. I had believed that to be a Christian I had to believe homosexuality was wrong. But I was starting to believe it was not a sin, so I was definitely in conflict and very scared.

"When I returned to Santa Barbara I was afraid to talk to anyone I knew about my changing beliefs. I decided that I didn't want to attend a church where gays were not welcome. I knew from my chaplaincy experience in San Francisco that the Episcopal Church was an open and inclusive church, so I decided to try Trinity. So here I am."

I look at Dodie. She looks at me. We move on.

Robin says she and Katrina live together in a "communal house." She, too, graduated from Westmont and is thinking about graduate school in education.

"I'm looking for a place to read the Bible and talk about it," she says softly. "I liked talking about it in school and since I graduated, I just haven't done it. But I don't want to talk about it in the same old way."

Mark Benson says he's going home for Christmas. "I don't know if you guys know this, but my father is a preacher. I'm a preacher's kid. He's an evangelical preacher—pretty fundamentalist, by our standards. He's a fair man, though."

Dodie grins. "I'm going back home for the first time since I got here and I'm wondering what I'm going to be like."

I report on my visit with Lois in the hospital. She's been in a week, after surgery to remove a tumor that's obstructing her bowel. When I entered her room, it was empty, and I was afraid. But I found her up on the roof, sitting on a deck in the sun, with two of her four children, her arm trailing IV tubes. I brought her a bunch of flowers from my garden and she thanked me and named them, one by one: "Roses, coreopsis, poppies, Canterbury bells, Mexican sage."

Then she asked after Kit.

"He's home from the hospital," I told her. "With Rande and the dogs, Here Boy and Rita. He planted an apricot tree so he will live to see it grow. He's getting ready to start chemo."

She winced. "Tell him it will be over soon."

ON SATURDAY, two days before Christmas, the grass around the church is wet and green from the winter rains, the ochre stone walls damp and bleeding. Teams of women in pale sweats and blue jeans work inside among aluminum stepladders, piles of greens, a crèche in mid-assembly. Iva Schatz, who grew up in an evangelical church and joined Trinity ten years ago, balances on a ladder and nudges a garland of greens hanging from a coat hanger across the smooth face of a stone column. Her daughter, Stefani, shouts commands from below. Near the altar, and at the back of the church, a forest of Scotch pines fills the air with sharp scent.

On his hands and knees, Bill La Voie, an architect with a boy's face and carrot hair, a former Roman Catholic who has recently arrived at Trinity, hangs tiny Christmas lights inside the crèche. He "borrowed" the lights from friends who are out of town. Later, as he places branches behind the crucifix hanging above the altar, an elderly man who has been a member at Trinity for twenty years marches into the church through the creaking sacristy door.

"What's the crucifix doing there?" he asks.

Ann Jaqua, who chairs the Worship Council, replies, "We've decided to leave it up this year, Peter."

"We've never done that before," Peter replies.

Outside in the children's play yard, four women stand amid piles of juniper, acacia, wire, and wreath forms.

"He was so controlling," says one. "No matter what I did, the decorations just weren't good enough."

"Don't tell me about controlling," adds another as she tucks an acacia branch into a half-moon of juniper. "My ex used to ask me why I did *everything* the way I did. I mean, when I cut my bread, he would ask me why do you do it *that* way."

Meanwhile, back in the church, Brother Laurence from Mount Calvary Monastery, a science teacher before he joined the order, has arrived to look around.

"Oh, I'm happy to see the crucifix," he says.

"Laurence," says Ann Jaqua, sweetly, "would you mind talking to Peter about the crucifix?"

"Sure," he says, turning to Peter.

"We've always taken it down at Christmas," Peter says.

"But it makes sense to keep it up," Laurence says kindly. "It's definitely part of the whole Christmas scene. Christ's death is present at his birth. Without it, Christmas doesn't mean as much."

"All you had to do," Peter says, turning on Ann, "was tell me why."

Dodie Little walks in, wearing black slacks and a luxurious black cashmere coat.

"I like the branches behind the crucifix," she says to Ann. "But don't you think they should be a little more symmetrical?"

"Bill did it," Ann replies. "I think that's how he wanted it."

"But don't you think you could ask him to put a branch over to the right and up?"

"No, I couldn't," Ann replies, placing a hand to her brow.

THE TREES, the greens, the ribbons, and the labor are all begged or borrowed. Trinity's budget for Christmas Eve, the biggest night of the year, is five hundred dollars to decorate a neo-Gothic building one hundred fifty feet long and fifty feet wide. The trees were purchased and donated by a local business (an usher works there as a manager). The scarlet poinsettias that line the altar were donated "in memory of . . ." or "in thanksgiving for . . ." by people who signed the ubiquitous church "sign-up sheets" at the "Welcome Table." Ann Jaqua has been sighted all week, sneaking through gardens, clippers in hand. Last night she made decorations for the tree at the back of the church under which people will place gifts for the Community Kitchen and the children at Transition House, a shelter for homeless families. As I walk in front of the altar, I see Ann standing next to Mark holding a roll of gold French ribbon she bought on sale last July. She mutters, "I'm going to make this place look like six Beverly Hills florists worked on it."

I LOOK OUT over the pews, at the army of volunteers, and at Ann and Mark. As my glance falls on them, he throws his head back, laughs a great horse laugh, and hugs her around her shoulders. I wonder to myself if he will stay. In the upcoming church year, at some point in "Ordinary Time," in the fall, Mark and the vestry will decide whether he will be called as our rector. After our rector resigned, Mark was offered the interim post in November, but his contract didn't begin until January. Last year at Christmas, we had no priest.

In the year before the former rector's resignation, gloom had settled on Trinity. I'd go to church and get out of there. Many times I wanted to leave the congregation altogether. It was as if we were part of a dysfunctional family: something was so wrong that to speak of it felt dangerous. One day Julius, the man who had first greeted me at Trinity's door, and I were opening cans of tomato paste in the kitchen; Julius turned to me and said, "The man in charge is never here."

On the other hand, laypeople were allowed to do things that might have run into resistance elsewhere: the soup kitchen flourished; the base community thrived. In these projects we were left alone, unattended but unencumbered.

The Episcopal Church doesn't have the same top-heavy hierarchy as does Rome, but a professionally trained clergy has resulted in a hierarchy nevertheless. Male Episcopal priests are still called "Father" in most parishes, and "Father knows best," is uttered, even now, with only half irony. (When Mark arrived at Trinity he said he didn't want to be called "Father" because women priests are rarely addressed as "Mother." Martha Siegel, the priest who helped organize the Thursday Night Eucharist at Trinity, says a colleague of hers in the Roman Catholic Church used to address her as "Mother Father.")

The duties of a priest include preaching, celebrating the Eucharist, hearing confessions, granting absolution, counseling, and teaching. But, of course, there is more to it than that. An Episcopal priest, like a Roman priest, is considered to be part of an apostolic succession and to have been called by God. Even someone like me, schooled in the rebellious sixties, salivates like Pavlov's dog a complicated mix of intimidated feeling and childlike desire for comfort when I see that white collar. To this day at Trinity, there are people who cannot call Mark by his first name.

Few priests are prepared to handle this provocative power. Many of them blow it. Clergy sexual misconduct is one extreme. A more common reaction is an isolated, authoritarian method of working—"fueled by anxiety," as one consultant put it.

It took three years to deal with the dysfunction at Trinity. During those years, the reputation of Trinity's laypeople ranged from "bold" to "troublemaking" in the diocesan offices. While Episcopal parishes are independent entities—priests are hired by vestries—the bishop nearly always has influence. Our bishop was divided in the case of Trinity. The parish was declining, a hefty earthquake retrofit had just been mandated by the city of Santa Barbara (estimated cost: $1.5 million), and a strong group of laypeople, including most of the vestry, wanted more dynamic leadership. On the other hand, stability is a key word in the Church, and priests can be forced out for all the wrong reasons. The bishop and his staff pressed Trinity's vestry to explore every option. Retired bishops, priests with degrees in psychology, committees of laypeople carrying sheaves of papers walked Trinity's halls wearing weary, bedside-manner smiles. Finally, after every avenue was exhausted, the situation changed when the rector resigned.

While a committee of the vestry searched for an interim priest, Trinity was left in the hands of laypeople. The officers of the vestry—the senior warden (a marvelously archaic term for something akin to president of the board), the junior warden, and the clerk—shouldered the liturgy. Kati Smith, the junior warden, who is the daughter of a priest, hunted retired or visiting clergy. The priests arrived on Sundays carrying their stoles and robes, vested in the sacristy, preached, celebrated the Eucharist, and left.

The rest of the week, we were on our own. Lou Smitheram, a cheerful librarian who had been at Trinity for forty-four years, found herself the senior warden.

"I didn't feel up to it intellectually. I was scared. I just skimmed by by my teeth," she said. "But people didn't leave, though we expected they might, and everyone contributed everything they could to the service: ushers went on and readers went on, without any pastoral supervision. I was a little surprised."

"What was amazing was that what I had seen as potential began to be realized," said Ann Jaqua. "The chips were down and the services went right on. What surprised me was, even though I knew there was a lot of untapped potential at Trinity, I thought that the gap between it and what we had to do was frighteningly huge. And then people came forward and said, 'Oh, sure I can do that. I've done that before.' People took on everything: they made sure we had preaching, the church stayed open, we paid the bills, the vestry met twice a month instead of once, and the soup kitchen kept going.

"I remember at one vestry retreat during that time, we did an exercise in imagining what Trinity could be, both to us and to the city. There was a lot of energy and excitement. Then we came up with something beautiful: Trinity could be a well, a source of strength and sustenance for us and for the city.

"The people who came up with this were unlikely people, they had never been high on my list. And I remember one of them, in sharing her vision, said she saw a lot of people coming but she didn't see a priest. I remember we all kind of nervously giggled."

IN THE MIDDLE AGES, the Church theoretically secluded itself from the world, separating the sacred and the secular, and adopted what it called *contemptus mundi*. Sometimes this was a liberating detachment, an abandonment of the world of wealth and corruption for voluntary poverty and prayer. At other times, however, the Church remained very much in the world, loving wealth and secular power, while at the same time treating the world with contempt.

This *contemptus mundi*, Thomas Merton believed, reflected the assumption that "theology had nothing to learn from the world and everything to teach the world." Its legacy is a Church that treats the laity as religious amateurs. "Laypeople," a priest hissed in my hearing, "are consumers of religion."

In those months we lived without a priest at Trinity, as laypeople held together a community of faith, we grew in worth and dignity. In the base communities, we were learning an adult form of theology, our own experiences reflected in the light of the Gospel, unmediated by "Father." It felt as if the membrane between Church and world was becoming more permeable.

"I realized today, working in the Kitchen," Ann Jaqua said at the base community one night, "that the serving table is like the table in the church, the altar. The two go together. I don't think the Eucharist makes sense without the soup."

She went on, "The community comes before the Eucharist because the community is the living thing in the moment, made up of bodies. Its work, its energy, its feelings, what everyone in it feels, thinks, hopes for, is the most important thing. We have come to believe that it is not, that our feelings as members of churches come second, after the Eucharist, after the sermon, after the form.

"The Church was originally designed, I think, to shape itself to us, not to force us to shape ourselves to it. In business they say, Either the people must shape themselves to fit the institution or the institution must shape itself to fit the people. We know more or less where most institutions stand."

Added Dodie, "In the Church, our lay ministry is never named or recognized. We are thanked, but never named."

As I listened to them, I thought about a parish I'd visited before I arrived at Trinity. It felt curiously out of touch: a comfortable club barricaded by insular language, a charismatic priest and a tight bond between members that didn't seem to translate to the world: a society worshipping itself, Durkheim said.

A college friend reported on another church, this one in Santa Fe, that felt attractive but finally irrelevant, a momentary safe haven.

"I'd go to church and I'd like it and I'd think, 'I'll sign up for this and that,' but when I got home I'd be glad I didn't," she said. "I realized it would just be a drain on my valuable time and nothing would really happen. It didn't feel like anyone actually believed that it could be transforming."

I began to wonder if this "irrelevance" was related to what we at Trinity were beginning to call the "ministry of laypeople." We chewed on it, even as the search committee looked for a priest. Then I picked up a book at a local bookstore, and I saw that at Trinity we were part of a larger group, part of a trend.

"People want good programs, inspiring worship, and meaningful ways of serving their faith," Clark Roof writes in *A Generation of Seekers: The Spiritual Journeys of Baby Boomers*. "But what does the church offer? All too often, we stick them on a committee. . . . Returning boomers often experience a gap between what they are looking for and what is offered to them by organized religion. Missing from many congregations is any real sensitivity to their deep religious concerns, or a structure designed to help people grow spiritually."

I wondered what such a structure would look like. The Roman Catholic Church, because of its shortage of priests, relies on laypeople, including many women, to run parishes, preach, distribute the Eucharist, and work as chaplains in hospitals and hospices. In the Episcopal Church, the role of laypeople is not so developed: part of the reason, ironically, is that Episcopal women may enter the priesthood, thus leaving the ranks of lay leaders.

Was the "structure" that would help people grow spiritually

greater participation in liturgy? Partly. But what would help people grow spiritually seemed to be about much more than technicalities, access to pulpits and Eucharist bread. It was about something else, something related to what Ann Jaqua had said at the base community: "The community is the living thing in the moment."

AS THE BASE COMMUNITY pondered lay ministry, the search committee began to clarify what sort of priest they wanted.

"We had a list of things," said Iva Schatz. "But more than anything, we realized we wanted a priest who would be totally inclusive. We had been on the cutting edge for the homeless in the Community Kitchen and Transition House, but we had never really had a priest who was actually *for* the marginalized; it had always been us pushing him. Our gay brothers and lesbian sisters were another part of that. Most of the candidates we interviewed hadn't really thought about this issue, or they hedged their bets."

A new name came up on the list, an executive with I. Magnin, returning to the priesthood after a ten-year absence. (Why the absence, I wondered.) The search committee liked their initial interview and invited him, in November, to preach. At one point in the sermon, not the best sermon I'd ever heard, Mark Asman talked about driving to the beach in his mother's Mustang convertible to surf, feeling cool, and then not being very good at it. In the middle of the sermon, I began to cry. I didn't know anymore what a priest was or was supposed to do, I realized, but I was tired of being without one. Then I thought, And he's tired of being without a parish. A small crowd collected around the search committee members at the coffee hour. They were all vigorously nodding their heads.

Under Mark's leadership this year, Trinity has not so much

changed as emerged; her wealth of talent and energy has been released. Watching Mark has been like observing the catalyst experiments we did in college: a platinum plate introduced to gaseous hydrogen and oxygen recombines them into water.

This spring Mark organized a "Lenten Series," potluck dinners followed by a program. I didn't like church potlucks then (in fact, I'd rather have died than attend one) but I was interested in the program, a video presentation by a professor of the Old Testament who writes on "prophetic imagination." When we arrived, covered dishes in hand, Mark started introducing us to one another.

"Nora," he said, "This is Margaret Vang. She's a retired social worker. She worked in mental health. I'll bet she'd be helpful with some of the problems you're running into at the Kitchen."

The tables were organized in a U shape, end to end. After an hour of dining and talking, we watched the video, discussed it for about twenty minutes, and left. The next Sunday, I greeted Margaret Vang by name.

As my college friend from Santa Fe said when I told her this story, "The point is he believed it would make a difference if you knew each other."

A month later Mark and a group of laypeople put on a tribute to George Barrett, a retired bishop who is a member at Trinity, on the sixtieth anniversary of his ordination. Bishop Barrett is a handsome, articulate man in his eighties with an air of goodwill, compassion, and keen judgment. Long a supporter of women, he ordained four women to the priesthood in Washington, D.C., in 1975, a year before it was "legal" in the Church. He was executive director of Planned Parenthood in Santa Barbara after his retirement. Once, when Mark preached on the need for inclusive language in liturgy and said, "You know, this is not goddess worship," George took me aside after the service and joked, "So, what's wrong with goddess worship?

"Seriously," he went on, "God is in and beyond the categories of male and female."

That night, the tables were full, funny poems were read, the mayor told a story about George's driving habits in the seventies ("He'd spot an Orange Julius juice stand on Highway 101 and just stop right in the middle of the freeway"), letters were read from bishops around the country. I stood in the back of the parish hall wondering why we had never known the full stature of this man in our midst.

Over tuna casseroles and Jell-O molds, we were slowly revealed to each other, as if we were uncovering a city buried in sand. Margaret began working in the soup kitchen; George preached. The door to the rector's office was always open. When the base community departed, the rector was there to say goodnight. When he baptized a baby, only weeks after he arrived, he carried the baby up and down the aisle to show her off.

He began to draw people into the center who had been at the margins, including me. Before I knew Mark well enough to watch him like a hawk, he asked me one day what I thought about Trinity's newsletter.

"It's dreadful," I replied. "It looks like something out of high school."

"Oh, really," he replied. "Well, now . . . what would you do about it?"

"Oh, I'd get a hot graphic designer to redesign it. Allison Jaqua, Ann's daughter. And I'd get Isabelle Walker-Klein, who's a journalist, to write a column and I'd assign different articles way ahead of time and I'd have a . . . oh, no," I said, but it was too late.

At a costume party for a parishioner's birthday, everyone

began making Mark try on various hats and masks. As I watched him gamely place a baseball cap on his head, followed by a Carmen Miranda pile of bananas and oranges, followed by a Groucho mustache, I thought to myself, They believe he belongs to them. A vestry member collected what she called Asmanisms and published them in the newsletter: "Let's make sure we're all on the same page," Mark often said at the beginning of a meeting, and "Hang on to your garter belts," and, my favorite, "You snooze, you lose."

This year Trinity feels less like "church" and more relevant, more connected to real life. The Thursday Night Eucharist has a feeling of raw openness, as if something might happen there, something new. We're experimenting with a Sunday school program based on the Montessori method. Children are asked to describe their own experience of God rather than mouth sentiments. Said Courtney Hall, an eight-year-old girl, this Advent, "Jesus is the trees, plants, air, bugs, and the whole world. Jesus is all that we wish to be."

When new people talk about why they picked Trinity, I see why I stayed. At "newcomers' orientations," each person mentions, in one way or another, that he or she wants to live out faith, in everyday life, not just in church. Many of them speak of wishing to come to church as they are, not in some cleaned-up or otherwise acceptable Sunday version.

"I want to bring my whole self to church," said a striking woman, a former actress in her thirties who is a practicing Buddhist. "I don't want to have to leave a part of my history or a piece of myself at the door."

As she spoke, I watched two young women sitting behind her cover each other's hands.

As Advent births the Christmas child, I see how our longing at Trinity is coming to fruition. Something is being born in all of us, including Mark.

"It wasn't until I came to Trinity that my theology went

from black and white to color," he said recently. "Partly, it was because I began therapy a few years before arriving here. Partly, it was because I was suddenly surrounded by laypeople who really taught me about lay ministry. For the first time, I had enough emotional health and balance to see the possibilities that one part talented laypeople and one part priest equals Church."

LATE IN THE AFTERNOON, I go home and open the last window on the Advent calendar. The tree is up. We bought it only a few days ago at a nursery, on sale. In the early evening, Vincent and I will dine, decorate the tree, and put luminarias—brown paper sacks with sand in the bottom and a votive candle inside—out on the sidewalk. Then I will go, alone, to midnight Mass while he remains, alone, at home. The first time it happened, we had just moved in together. Vincent's family came to our house for dinner on Christmas Eve. At ten o'clock, as I put on my coat to go to Mass, Vincent's mother said sadly, "Oh, I thought you lived here, too."

Raised in the Roman Catholic Church, Vincent shares, with a multitude, a complex inheritance. As a boy he believed in the doctrines of the Church: the Trinity, the virginity of Mary, transubstantiation. Then, radicalized in his adolescence, he decided they weren't true, but were instead things that human beings had constructed. Yet Vincent is sometimes still a Roman Catholic in his heart. The Roman Church, as everyone must know, is far more than a church: it's a family, a culture, a whole country of its own. While at odds with the Catholic tradition, he respects it and has a deep suspicion of church reform. Mystified by my desire for more inclusive language in the liturgy, he says, "I liked it when it was in Latin."

Like many of my friends who don't attend a church,

Vincent doesn't know of many changes in theology, liturgy, or ethics in the last twenty years, in either the Roman or the Episcopal Church. When he attacks some part of the Church, he's often attacking something that doesn't exist anymore. Part of the reason is that changes in religion are meaningless to him; part is that the Church and the media are equally bad at publicizing religion or religious concerns; and part is that he remains rooted in the past, when the Church was the air he breathed.

This makes our mixed marriage "challenging" as they say. I am often scarified into silence. Yet in the brief moments when we risk the words that might bridge the gulf between us, I find my language pushed out of an easy, insular code.

One afternoon, Vincent and I were driving home from the gym. "When I was writing a poem every morning, it took a lot of energy," Vincent said. "What I would call my writing energy. It cut it down. But now that I am not writing a poem every morning, I tend to forget who I am during the day. The least little thing blows me away."

"That's exactly what it's like for me when I don't pray," I replied. "It is like a fragmentation. I fragment more easily."

At dinner one night, Vincent and Andrew Colquhoun, from Mount Calvary Monastery, sat across the table from each other and struggled with the need to find, not a common language for spiritual experience, but a way to hear each other without erosion or erasure.

"Many of us don't agree with the old language or find in it a complete description of our life with God," Andrew said. "Even those of us in the Church.

"When I joined the Episcopal Church," he continued, "I would say that the Sacrament, because it goes beyond words or concepts, was the only thing that could suffice because the words had become empty."

"I may have had what you call a mystical experience," Vincent said, "when I saw *The Night Watch*, the painting by Rembrandt, in the Rijksmuseum in Amsterdam. I was struck on the one hand by its grandeur and on the other hand by the extraordinary humanity of the faces. *The Night Watch* is part of a series of paintings of groups of home guards, who were like the National Guard. Most of the portraits show people at banquets, eating, but this painting shows people getting ready for battle. There is an ironic quality to it, sort of an absurdity to what they're doing, but it's so gentle. There are deep, deep spaces in the painting, deep chambers, so that it never seems to end. The absurdity of what they're doing is counterbalanced by the depth and darkness of those chambers. When I saw the painting I burst into tears.

"Why I think this would be akin to a mystical experience is because the response I had was very complicated but all at once. It was not a sequence, it was this tremendously complicated idea, with so powerful a feeling to it, and it happened all at once."

Andrew was silent for a minute. Then he said, "When I was on Iona several years ago, I went to a service in the abbey led by men and women in their twenties. A young woman with a punk haircut led the procession. The service was about South Africa. It was very moving to me. I'm not sure why. I ended up just bawling in the middle of it. Then afterward I went off by myself to the prayer corner in the south aisle. I felt spent. I closed my eyes. And I felt these hands touching me, gently, hands comforting me. And I thought, 'This is the communion of saints.' "

WHEN I SIDLE in the side door at ten-thirty, the church is almost full. Mark Benson motions me to sit with him, gestures to his watch, and whispers, "God will be here in ninety minutes."

He's all dressed up in a dark suit and gray silk tie. As I sneak a look around, I see Elizabeth Reifel in a dove-gray silk coat, Ann Jaqua in black velvet. The church itself is dressed up: gold ribbon and greens adorn the columns, poinsettias fill the altar area, in the corners are the tall green pines. As if six Beverly Hills florists had worked on it.

The procession begins at the back of the church. We stand and sing, "O come, all ye faithful." The priests' robes are gold and white.

Mark Benson walks to the pulpit to read Paul's letter to Titus: "For the grace of God has appeared, bringing salvation to all. . . ."

Mark Asman reads the Gospel: "In those days a decree went out from Emperor Augustus that all the world should be registered."

In his sermon, he says, "As I look around this room tonight, I am reminded of the complexities and challenges of our lives. I am reminded of the families that have been blessed with the great joy that enters into their midst with the birth of a child. I am reminded of casual but poignant conversations alluding to the loneliness of lost families during this seemingly happy season. And I am reminded of who isn't here. The homeless men who wait in the shadows for us to leave this place tonight so they can roll out their sleeping bags on our porch. I am reminded of the men just a few blocks away, struggling for their lives filled with AIDS, who have suffered the great pains of rejection by family and Church. I am reminded of the men and women of Transition House . . ." He goes on to quote from an article by Jeff Dietrich, long a leader of the Los Angeles Catholic Worker.

"In his ministry, Jesus healed a great number of sick people. But these miraculous healings were not cures in the literal sense of the word so much as they were healings of a breach in the social environment. A disabled person who lives in a loving, supportive environment does not necessarily need to experience actual physical regeneration in order to feel a sense of wholeness. Jesus' healings were a sign of reconciliation and acceptance of those who had been shunned by the dominant culture. It was the moral righteousness of the religious and political elites that resulted in sickness and death for the rejected."

After the sermon, midway through the service, Mark says, "The peace of the Lord be always with you." We reply, "And also with you."

As we wish one another peace, two women I don't recognize shake my hand. One of them reaches around and gently tucks in the label of my dress.

We sing a nineteenth-century carol, "The snow lay on the ground, the stars shone bright. . . ."

Before he begins the Eucharist prayer, Mark invites everyone to communion. "Wherever you are in your journey of faith," he says, "you are welcome at this table."

Anne Howard and I stand together to the left of the altar to serve. Below the hem of her white robe, red cowboy boots shine. We just stand there and they come. On the faces of the many strangers in line is a guarded hope. A bearded man almost grabs the cup from my hands. Ann Jaqua's daughter Jennifer and her fiancé, Raphael, visiting from Texas, arrive in front of us. They are like two horses, beautiful and sleek, without guile. A parishioner with HIV, Ben Hitz and Lois—just released from the hospital—Katrina, Robin. A woman bent over. A man with a fierce, angry frown. The painter Alice Neel said about the subjects of her portraits that they assumed a pose that demonstrated "what the world has done to them and their retaliation." One by one, they sip from the cup.

I move into the place where each person becomes all there is, as if he or she were a hologram for the world. The little girl from the Catechesis Sunday School, Courtney, reaches up toward the cup and I bend down. Her face is openly expectant; she knows what she wants. Just before she sips, she looks into me and I feel my guard fall away and my heart open. She has given me communion.

As Anne and I carry the remaining Sacrament back to the sacristy, Anne whispers to me, "It's a privilege."

Finally, we sing "Silent Night" and the Mass is over. All of us are putting on our coats, wishing each other a Merry Christmas. I see Mike, the Kitchen's janitor, standing outside with his bedroll. "Merry Christmas," he says as I walk to my car. I feel a drag on my shoes, as if they were weighted. I turn around. Only Mark Asman's car is left in the parking lot. He's standing in the hallway, turning out lights, when I walk back in.

"Can Mike and his girlfriend spend the night inside tonight?" I ask him.

Mark looks out the door at the figure standing on the porch.

"Tonight of all nights," he replies, and gestures to Mike to come in.

Epiphany

SOMETIMES IT'S AS IF I were living in two worlds, but
more often it's as if each world challenged and sanctified the
other. I can dimly see something coming into existence, at
the periphery of the eye. It is like the voices I once heard in the
Ceremonial House, one of the Jewish museums in Prague. The
House is adjacent to the Old Jewish Cemetery, the second-
oldest cemetery in Europe, where old and new gravestones sit
on top of one another, crowded as teeth. In the House are
drawings made by children from Terezín, the village near the
northern Czech border that the Nazis turned into a transport
camp for Jews. Some of the drawings are of children threatened by dark shapes, monsters, or bolts of lightning. Others
are the kinds of drawings—butterflies, a tree with grass—that
contemporary parents might attach to the refrigerator with a
magnet and then throw away or toss in a drawer with other
keepsakes; but these are permanent, encased in glass, because
the children are dead. Among them, people are silent, but alert
as if listening, because it is as if the children are speaking. I
knew they were speaking and it seemed to me that everyone around me knew and we felt that if we just listened hard
enough, we could make out the words.

That is how it is when I hear God speaking, when I see
what could be or even what is, but too dimly to make it out. I
can almost hear, I can almost see. I can almost touch the peace

proclaimed. Sometimes I think that faith is only about increasing peripheral vision, peripheral hearing.

Epiphany: the season of the weird. It starts on January 6, twelve days after Christmas, when the Magi, three foreign kings or astronomers or both, arrive at Jesus' cradle bearing an odd assortment of gifts: gold, for a king; frankincense, an incense; and myrrh, the fragrant ointment used to anoint the dead.

Two more stories are told in Epiphany: John's baptism of Jesus at the river Jordan, and the miracle at the wedding in Cana. The Magi follow a new star; a dove descends; water turns to wine. In each of the stories, the singularity of Jesus is revealed, as if it were rising to the surface from under water. Events bring into focus what has been at the periphery. I see in Jesus his own dawning sense of what God has in store for him, and for him alone. If it is true for Jesus, I realize in this season, then it is true for me.

I spend the day of Epiphany with my best friend, Cynthia, at her grandmother's apartment in San Francisco, helping her choose what to keep, what to give to Goodwill. A week ago, Cynthia's grandmother, *Abuelita*, as she was called by her grandchildren, told the young doctor who said she would have to have surgery for her stomach that she had no intention of doing any such thing, and died that night in her sleep.

Cynthia is Jewish and Mexican on her father's side; her mother was Episcopalian. Cynthia, partly in an effort to mediate between the two, is an agnostic. When Cynthia and I met in 1974, I was not a churchgoer and never spoke about my unresolved feelings and thoughts about God, about faith, about church. When I suddenly returned to church in 1979, it was a jolt to her. Once she cried on the telephone: "What if you become someone I don't understand? What if you can only talk to people who believe what you believe?"

The day after Epiphany, she and I rise early and drive to a hill behind Berkeley and hike, vigorously, for eight miles, looking down on the cities below, the fog, and the towers of the Golden Gate Bridge.

"Do you believe that Jesus was the son of God?" she asks me. "The only son?" I reply that there must have been something amazing about him, but that I am not sure even he knew what it was.

"What about people who believe other things, who follow other faiths?"

"All that Jesus said," I reply, "is to love God, love others, and forgive your enemies. If you do these things, you'll have eternal life. Eternal life is not a reward in heaven for being good; it's what you experience when you really love. People of other faiths who practice loving certainly must experience the same thing."

"Then why be a Christian rather than a Muslim or a Buddhist?"

"Because the story is compelling to me." I hesitate, then I go on. "And because I do believe in the Incarnation. I want to believe that God intervenes."

ON THURSDAYS, I continue to work in the soup kitchen. Ephraim is there for a few hours one day, singing rock songs and generally getting in the way. He panhandles me before he leaves—a virtual taboo in the Kitchen; most of the men we serve abhor begging. I refuse him, rudely, and begin to turn away. His face falls, I see it out of the corner of my eye, and I want to apologize—I can say no without being nasty—but Peter calls out to me from the dishwashing room. By the time I turn around again, Ephraim is gone.

A woman dressed in a brown sweater and one of the volunteer aprons swaggers into the Kitchen. She has a lovely, intelligent face, but something about her is off; her body is a lump under the apron and sweater and her expression drills holes in my chest. I ask her nervously if she wants something and she replies, "You sound like a social worker." I'm suddenly furious, the anger rising so fast I envision steam coming out of my ears. She has found me out: I did sound exactly like a stereotypical social worker, fear covered by false cheer. Then she takes off her apron and throws it at me. Peter comes out of the dish-washing room and tells her she has to go outside. We both walk toward her. She backs away, muttering, and I follow her to the door. At the door, she pauses, then snaps, "You're responsible for Vietnam and the drop in the Mexican peso."

Back in the kitchen, I tell Ann Jaqua.

"Well, that solves that mystery," she replies.

We are visited the next week by a crazy African-American preacher from Louisiana. He arrives at the Kitchen, trailing his thin beautiful wife and their child. He has just moved his family here, he says as he takes a bowl of soup from my hands. He plans to preach on the streets. Then he tells me to go home and read Jeremiah 1:4–8. I feel silly, but I do it. The passage reads in part, "Now the words of the Lord came to me saying, 'Before I formed you in the womb I knew you, and before you were born I consecrated you; I appointed you a prophet to the nations.' "

He returns a few days later. I give him lunch. His wife looks healthier; the child asks for grapes. The preacher begins to rave: "The husband and the wife nearly broke up yesterday," he says. "The husband got bad, angry. But we had a prayerful, we prayed."

"Hello, Reverend," I say.

"What is your name?" he asks. "What is your name?"

I tell him.

"Did you read the passage that I gave you?"

"Yes," I reply.

"That's you," he says. "That's you." I am secretly delighted. A few days later, a pious deacon who is also working in the Kitchen tells me that a preacher told her to read Jeremiah. I feel like a fool, then laugh. The whole episode never leaves me.

At the base community early in February, Lois Hitz describes mushroom hunting in a canyon behind Santa Barbara. This year, we've had extraordinary rains, floods in fact, that have left the hills green and sliced with rushing creeks. Lois and her companions wore hip boots as they rooted for the precious chanterelle, a beautiful yellow mushroom that tastes like veal.

"They would be under the leaves around the oak trees," she says with a hunter's pleasure. "First we'd see just the rim showing and then this incredible yellow, fluted cone. We gathered them in paper bags and took them down to the picnic tables at Sheffield Park and spread them out. I thought I had never seen anything so beautiful." As she speaks, the whole of her life funnels into this story; her gratitude for having had this moment fills the room. At the end, almost as an aside, she says that the doctors are "chasing" her cancer.

Nancee says she's been reading the story of Jonah. "It's such an odd, interesting story," she says. "I like his stubbornness."

Elizabeth reports that she has "moments" when she understands "something about grace."

Katrina says she'd like to pass, then changes her mind. "At our house," she says, "where I live, we have a group therapy meeting each week. I told them about this base community last week. I live in this house because just before I graduated from Westmont, I was hospitalized for depression." She stops, then looks across the table at Dodie who has made a soft, involuntary cry.

I report that my brother Kit has begun chemotherapy. He lies in a room for three hours every ten days with an IV dripping platinum into his veins. Antinausea pills help him not to vomit, but he is so debilitated he can't get off the couch, and then his body aches so badly he screams. "They are nearly killing me," he whispers on the phone, "in order to kill the cancer."

I see our stories as fragments, salvaged by their telling.

We read together the story of the wedding at Cana. At a festival wedding feast, Jesus and his friends are guests. The partying has been going on for days and, finally, the host runs out of wine. Jesus is asked by his mother to do something about it. At first, he is irritated—"What has this to do with me?" he asks her. Then he relents. Six stone jugs, used for purification rituals, are filled with water. "Now draw some out," Jesus says. "And take it to the chief steward." The steward tastes the water that has become wine and says to the bridegroom, "You have kept the good wine until now."

"What does this story say to us tonight?" Ann Jaqua asks, and she answers. "What I'm hearing is that we are asked to turn something ordinary, something like water, into something full of life. We are asked to take ourselves—our ordinary souls and bodies—to be a 'living sacrifice,' as the Book of Common Prayer says, to make of our own ordinariness something fully alive."

WHEN I RETURNED to church in 1979, I did not know why. I was and am an ordinary person with ordinary concerns. I'm an ordinary member of my generation. But I am almost always the only practicing Christian at a dinner party, often the only "religious" person, certainly the only one who attends a church regularly, believes in God, prays, has a denomination. Throughout much of the eighties, I knew this about myself in secret and never mentioned it to anyone outside the Church, as if I were gay and still in the closet.

The cause of my secrecy was largely embarrassment. I feared being thought of as fundamentalist or stupid or both. From the time I started attending church again in my late twenties to my middle thirties, I kept my secret. While my friends, including Cynthia, knew I went to Mass, we rarely spoke about it. To be fair, I didn't know how to speak about it. My faith at the beginning wasn't coherent: what words came out were sentimental, defensive, distorted, like bulbs that bloom too early and are bitten by frost.

In the beginning, I would go to church and cry. I spent a year crying in church. I couldn't say the Nicene Creed. I refused to pledge, to promise a monthly sum to the church. I made myself as invisible as possible in the church, and the church, an upper-class parish in Pacific Heights in San Francisco, took little notice of me. I did kneel at the rail with the other communicants and take the Sacrament. Then I returned to my pew, to kneel and cry again. Very often, I didn't know what I was doing there. Many layers of feeling, experience, and habit had to come together before I understood religious faith, including my own. I felt at first as if I were learning a new language or how to dance: I was so awkward and foolish that at every turn I wanted to quit.

Why did I cry so much? Apparently, many people who return to church or discover it later in their lives end up crying in the pews. At the time I understood my tears psychologically—that is, I understood them to be about something unresolved in myself—and I took myself to a therapist. Now I understand those tears both psychologically and religiously—different ways of understanding, or different when the psychological is understood to be about something one can fix, rather than about something one can make room for. A friend of mine, a writer, once said he had no gift for religion. A friend of his, a believer, told him not to worry, God would find him. In religious terms, I was lost and on the verge of being found.

I loved the ritual, the cross held high before the lines of choir, the swinging incense, the bowing and kneeling. I loved the liturgy of the Episcopal Church: each week, each Mass, the same form, from the Book of Common Prayer. Each Sunday morning the service began with a hymn, then the opening acclamation, said by the priest: "Blessed be God: Father, Son, and Holy Spirit." To which the people responded, "And blessed be his kingdom, now and forever. Amen." Then what is called the Collect of Purity: "Almighty God, unto whom all hearts are open, all desires known, and from whom no secrets are hid. Cleanse the thoughts of our hearts. . . ."

The trouble was, I didn't believe that it was about anything real. I went to church as if it were a ballet. I went to the ballet on Sunday, felt many different kinds of feelings, couldn't bring those feelings into line with my intellect or figure out how to integrate them into my own experience, and so gradually they faded as the week wore on. It didn't connect. I suspect that many people who faithfully attend church remain in such a state and don't know what to do about it. (And those who watch us from the outside wonder, rightly, What's the point of all this?) What I finally understood was that simply going to church doesn't do it, but neither does not going to church.

It takes a long time to understand what is being asked, and who is doing the asking. Part of the problem is that we do not want to hear the voice or understand the message. In a sermon at Mount Calvary Monastery, Roy Parker, a lean monk whose running shoes poke out from beneath his robes, said that the presence of God was like a bit he'd seen on *Candid Camera*. The camera crew had arranged a large terra-cotta pot next to a table in a restaurant. In the pot was a trick plastic plant that would "grow" suddenly when someone sat down. A woman arrived and was seated.

"So she's sitting there and the cameras are on her and suddenly the plant starts growing and she looks at it, bug-eyed, and then she looks furtively around, as we all might do, to see if anyone else has seen it and when she sees that they haven't—they are just eating and talking—she moves to another table.

"When we are visited by grace," Roy concluded, "and everyone else is just eating and talking, we tend to move to another table."

That year, I was torn between dealing with God and my own habit of moving to another table.

In 1982, Vincent and I moved to Colorado. There I attended St. Lawrence's Mission, a small church in the mountains outside Denver. I remember the first time I found that church, on Easter Sunday, in a VFW hall up a dirt road in the middle of a field. A hundred people were there, on the big day of the Christian year, and they seemed a population typical of the small towns on the eastern slope of the Rockies. Most of the women wore faded dresses; the money had been spent on the children's Easter outfits. The men wore dull gray or brown polyester pants with coats too tight across the back and bright white shirts. A woman I was sure represented "the person on whose pledge the church depends" sat near the front on a folding brown chair; she had on a red velvet coat and a ruffled white shirt. The priest, Larry Donoghue, a man in his forties, had a soft, intelligent face and sprigs of curly hair just turning gray. He asked for newcomers to raise their hands and stand up after the service was over, and when I grudgingly rose to my feet, everyone clapped and smiled.

In that little church, I began to understand "the community of faith," how, like your family, it presents you with people you would not normally choose. In his essay "Limited Engagements," Philip Turner, a former dean at Yale Divinity School, says we become members of a family or "household," which serves in part as a cure for loneliness. "Once baptized, each person is given both family and friends in such a way that the terrible problem of human loneliness is, in principle, overcome by incorporation into God's family." Turner adds, "To the extent that the church recommends its traditional teaching and yet at the same time fails to be a family in which loneliness is remedied, it will fail to recognize the necessary framework for understanding its own teaching. . . . What we need to form is a moral and political community which is something more than a lonely crowd in pursuit of private ends."

We later moved the church to the back of a restaurant. When we took communion, we could hear the families eating pancakes through the wall. Because it was a marginal mission, with no building to keep up, most of our extra money went to the outreach committee. The outreach committee, in turn, paid people's electric bills in the winter when the temperature dropped below zero nine days out of ten. When it came time to vote on whether we would build an actual church, I voted against it.

Shortly after we moved to Colorado, Vincent and I were married. We had a potluck wedding at a ranch in Sonoma, in California, on a September day when the temperature must have risen to 103. Bill Barcus, a priest from my old church in Pacific Heights, officiated at the service. A week before our wedding, Vincent and I met with him in San Francisco in his tiny study at the church. He pulled out the 1552 Prayer Book, and we deleted most of the references to Jesus, at Vincent's request. ("The Father, the Blip, and the Holy Spirit," said my friend Ellen Meloy.) I went along, unsure of my own feelings about Jesus, happy that Vincent was agreeing to the Anglican service at all. We left in the earthy language that was excised in later prayer books, "With this ring I thee wed, with my body I thee worship."

We lived in Colorado for two years, through the worst winters in a century, and yearned in earnest for California. In February of '84, we were offered jobs at Patagonia, an outdoor clothing company near Santa Barbara. Vincent was already at work, at a trade show, and so the whole church helped me move. I remember how easy it was with so many people to help.

I tried to find a place in Santa Barbara that resembled that mission church, and failed. I started attending Friday morning Mass at Mount Calvary Monastery, where I met Dan Corrigan, Ann Jaqua, Mark Grotke, and a variety of people I often thought of as resembling those in a Graham Greene novel. Finally, late in the eighties, I began attending Sunday services at Trinity. I felt as if I were just on the edge of something, about to see, about to hear. When it happened, it happened very suddenly.

One day in 1989 I walked in the door from a trip to San Francisco and answered the phone. The woman on the other end had a strong voice that cracked at the higher registers. I realized she was elderly but so strong that her age was not immediately evident. Alice McGrath, who was then seventy-one, invited me to go to Nicaragua on a ten-day tour with eleven other women. The Sandinistas were still in power. I, who never make a decision regarding travel until the last possible minute, said yes.

Why a trip to a small country in the midst of a waning revolution charged up my religious life is a story not even I completely understand. Yet Nicaragua was fully real to me; each person and circumstance was magnified and heightened as they are after a death. Our group of women—lawyers, a personnel director, a CEO, and journalists—stepped off the ancient jet in Managua into air so steamy it was like walking into a laundry. Parrots played in the cashew trees over the patio tables at our hotel. The bed mattresses were one and a half inches thick, on old iron beds with springs like those at summer camp. The water was turned on twice a day. There was no hot water. I got to know a Spanish phrase very well— *"No hay,"* "There is none." At the hospital, there was no aspirin. Children with severe diarrhea lay on cots hooked up to IVs; their mothers sat beside them. At the theater where we watched a rehearsal of *Waiting for Lefty*, there was no soap, no toilet paper, no water.

What there *was*, however, was profound and elusive. It was like nothing I had expected. It was like Orwell's account of Barcelona in December 1936, when the anarchists had briefly taken over the city. "It was the first time that I had ever been in a town where the working class was in the saddle. . . . Waiters and shop walkers looked you in the face and treated you as an equal. Servile and ceremonial forms of speech had temporarily disappeared. Nobody said, 'Señor,' or 'Don' or even 'Usted'; everyone called everyone else 'Comrade' and 'Thou' and said 'Salud' instead of 'Buenos Dias.' . . . Except for a small number of women and foreigners there were no 'well-dressed' people at all. . . . There was much in it that I didn't understand, in some ways I did not even like it, but I recognized it immediately as a state of affairs worth fighting for."

It was not anything as simple as "life under socialism" or "the victory of the proletariat." Nor was it quite like Orwell. (After all, it was 1989 and I came from California, where you might wish that waiters would *not* treat you as an equal.) But the fall of a hierarchy has vast consequences. What I began to see was that although Nicaragua might be many things, it was a place where people written off elsewhere—people who might elsewhere not even be thought to exist—had been joined to the body politic, were valued and worthy. Our guide was a young man named Daniel Ramírez. One night he told the story of his life as we stood in the courtyard of our hotel drinking flat Nicaraguan beer and smoking Marlboros bootlegged from El Salvador. At first glance at the airport, Daniel had struck me as a hustler and I hadn't liked him much. But as the days went by, he grew on me. He taught us Des Moiches, a complicated game with more rules than bridge—a new rule seemed to be added every hand—and he won almost every game. When he won he leaned back in his chair, threw his head back, and raised his fists over his head in unself-conscious (and very unsocialist) glee.

In the seventies, before the revolution, he had been a troubled teenager in Managua. Unable to cope with him anymore, his mother sent him to live with his father in San Francisco. There, he became, as he said, a *cholo*, a hoodlum. I, too, was living in San Francisco at the time; Ramírez told me that if I had seen him then, in the Mission district, I would have been repelled by him. "You would have gone, 'Ugh,' " he said. "I mean, I was bad. I would have ended up in prison or in the cemetery. Or . . ." He made a motion with his finger against his arm as if sliding a needle into his vein.

Ramírez decided to return home—an aunt had made him a standing offer to pay his airfare back to Nicaragua—and so, only a few months after the revolution in 1979, he returned to Managua. He was still a *cholo* and people in Managua said "Ugh" when they passed him on the street. He taught his friends dances from the United States and hung out until he got bored. Then, Ramírez said, "I joined the literacy campaign." He glanced at me quickly. "I actually joined it, basically, to get laid." But as he taught children and grandmothers the alphabet, Ramírez said, "I began to feel useful, really, for the first time in my life. I began to turn my life around. The revolution saved my life."

Much later in the trip, I met a woman in the ladies' lounge at the Popular Theater. She was a buxom blond woman in her fifties, dressed in tight-fitting white jeans and a pale green tank top. Strings of imitation gold necklaces hung around her neck. We stood together in front of the sink. I reached for the nonexistent soap and then turned on the water faucet only to hear the fwoosh of escaping air.

"No hay," she said sympathetically. I nodded and we chatted

for a while, comparing notes on what was not in Nicaragua: eye liner, mascara, pantyhose, penicillin. Then I asked her where she was from.

"Uruguay," she replied. "But I have come here from Sweden. My husband and I were arrested in Uruguay. We were in prison seven years. We were exiled to Sweden. Now we have come back to here."

"Why did you leave Sweden to come here?" I asked.

"Because one person counts here," she replied. "One person doesn't count in Sweden."

When I returned to Santa Barbara, everywhere I looked, the people who had been either invisible to me or a quaint backdrop to this tourist town were suddenly real: the Latino gardener on the street with his leaf blower, the dishwasher in the back room of a restaurant, the old man sitting at the bus stop.

I was shaken. I no longer wished to live as I had been living—working, eating, tending my marriage, dropping in on church. I wanted to have something to do with what I had seen in Nicaragua because I knew that it was a glimpse of something else. I didn't want to join the revolution or become a Marxist or say, as a depressed-looking fellow said at a fund-raiser, *"Soy Sandinista."* If it can be put into words, what I yearned for was to embody my shaky faith, to feel my faith in my flesh, acted out, incarnate. Said W. H. Auden about the goal of psychoanalysis: "To free the patient from the slavery of impersonal behavior so that he may become capable of personal deeds. A deed is an act by which the doer voluntarily discloses himself to others." To make, of an event, an experience.

Men and women before me had walked down this road and through what Jesus once called "the narrow gate." Wealthy young St. Francis sealed his conversion by kissing a leper on the mouth; Dorothy Day went to live in the slums of New York and founded the Catholic Worker; Simone Weil worked in factories to be with those she called "the despised layers of social hierarchy." Lines from one of Paul's letters to the Corinthians kept running through my head: "God has chosen things low and contemptible, mere nothings, to overthrow the existing order." I thought, What if those words are about something real? What if they are a hint about the kingdom? A hint about God? What if this religion I've been practicing and this Gospel I've rarely read, but heard from the priest every Sunday, is not a metaphor but a description of reality?

I thought I would end up returning to Nicaragua. Instead, I went to work in the soup kitchen. In the Kitchen, slowly, things came apart and then took on shape. "Are you willing to be un-formed?" a priest asked me.

One particular day in the Kitchen, I was tired and irritated; my stomach hurt and I'd had a flat tire on the way to the church. I'd been there only a matter of minutes when Sam, the sexton, walked up to me and said that the woman who threatens people was in the bathroom. He stood in front of me, waiting.

"So?" I said.

"So, you're supposed to call the police," he replied.

The ladies' lounge is one of the most comfortable rooms in the church: a sunny white room with an old green leatherette couch and matching armchair, two wide mirrors, and long leaded-glass windows. (To one of the mirrors someone has taped this note: "Objects in the mirror appear larger than they really are.") "The woman who threatens people" was seated on the couch with her tray in front of her when we came in. She was a young woman, possibly in her thirties, with prematurely gray hair tucked under a knitted red cap. Her reputation arose from several incidents in which she threatened to hit people on the street. The social workers in town worried about what her behavior could evoke—some guy might take her seriously and beat her up—more than they were concerned about what harm she might do.

I said hello and she nodded. I sat down.

"Your social workers have asked us to call the Mental Health Team when you come here," I said to her. "They want to talk to you. I would like to call them."

Without hesitation, she replied, "You don't have my permission to make that call."

I looked down at my hands on my knees, and said, "Well, that's that," and stood up to leave.

Outside, I told Sam and the church secretary, crowded together in the office, that I wasn't calling the police. "She's not doing anything," I said weakly. They looked at me with contempt.

Back in the dining room, a small homeless woman with dark red hair, careful makeup, bright lipstick, and a tilt to her head asked me if a woman was in the bathroom. Yes, I replied.

"I want to go speak to her," she said.

"Oh, I don't think that's too good an idea," I said, imagining two volatile women fighting on the floor of the bathroom and a member of the Episcopal Church Women waiting to pee.

"I can go in there if I want to, you can't stop me," she said, and stalked off across the dining room. I followed her, thinking nasty thoughts about the homeless, the insane, and people in general, but all she did was turn around and sit back down, throwing me a scowl.

"Francis from the Montessori School called to say someone has tied up a dog in the alley near the kids' play yard," Sam said.

I peered out the back door. The dog was there, a nice black dog sitting happily in the middle of the walkway. Sam announced it to the dining room; no one responded. He and I walked out to chat with the dog.

"I know who she belongs to," Sam said cheerfully. "The guy that's real belligerent."

Thanks a lot, Jesus, I thought, as I untied the dog, walked her to the front lawn, and tied her up again. It fell to me to tell her owner, a big, bearded guy in a wheelchair with red rummy's eyes.

Sitting down next to him, I told him I'd moved his dog to the front lawn because we couldn't have dogs tied up near the kids. He looked worried. "I've tied her up again," I assured him. "Oh, okay," he said, and returned to his conversation.

Just then, the red-haired woman stood up, marched over to the serving line, and yelled at one of the volunteers from the Presbyterian Church.

"I bet you play with yourself at night because you don't have anyone to sleep with, you're too fat."

I thought, Uh-oh, too close to home.

I walked toward her. Peter, the dishwasher, came up behind me. She started backing across the room. "Don't come near me."

Peter moved toward her. "You've got to go outside now."

A big guy sitting at a table near us said, "Don't do that to her. Just leave her alone, she'll leave."

I said to Peter, "Let's take his advice."

Peter walked away and she left. I walked back to the serving line and breathed in two breaths, looked up and saw her standing in the doorway of the office, gesturing with her hands. I walked through the doors and into the office and tried the first thing that came to my mind.

"Would you come outside with me?"

"Okay," she said.

We went outside. She started to rant.

"Do you know who I am? I have a résumé in my suitcase. I'm somebody. I'm not homeless. I have a nice place. Did you hear what she said to me?"

In a flash, I heard my own words—furious, helpless, outraged—at a clerk in a store or a medical insurance employee:

"Do you know who I am!" I felt for her, just as I felt, suddenly, for myself.

"You feel offended and insulted. I know just how you feel," I said, and for once, I wasn't lying.

Her eyes bugged out. She said, "Yes, I feel offended and insulted," as if tasting the words on her tongue. "Yes, I do." Then: "They won't let me have dessert here."

"I'll make sure you have dessert."

"Thank you," she said.

"Thank you for coming to lunch."

We shook hands.

Inside the door, Peter was standing next to his bicycle, about to leave.

"I wasn't much help to you today," he said gently. I put my arms around his neck.

"No, you weren't," I said and, again, I wasn't lying. "But you are usually a lot of help."

Mark Asman hurried out of his office, carrying a sheaf of papers.

"She sounded just like me," I said to him.

"Scary, isn't it," he replied.

THESE WERE MY EPIPHANIES: no thunderclaps, no voices from heaven. A brief glimpse, a sense of release, and the world was righted, remade in a way that was upside-down from what I had imagined. Though I still didn't count on these moments, I came to the point where I noticed them.

In "The Production of the World," John Berger continues:

We are taught to oppose the real to the imaginary, as though one were always at hand and the other distant, far away. And this opposition is false. Events are always at hand. But the coherence of these events—which is what we mean by reality—is an imaginative construction. Reality always lies beyond, and this is as true for materialists as for idealists, for Plato and for Marx. Reality, however one interprets it, lies behind a screen of clichés. Every culture produces such a screen, partly to facilitate its own practices (to establish habits) and partly to consolidate its own power. Reality is inimical to those with power.

Ann Jaqua calls God "the Really Real." Now I saw what I was after; I sought what lay beyond the screen of clichés. Hidden in the corridors of power, it was revealed among the marginal. I was learning things in the soup kitchen I could not learn anywhere else.

I BEGAN TO PRAY every day, although I didn't know how. I began to notice the connection between prayer and activity in the world. And I felt, in the end, an uncanny sense that all of this was happening because of a hand held against my back.

Candidates for the priesthood often talk about being "called." I used to cringe at that word; I found it overblown for what was, I thought, a career choice. Are bankers called? I'm still wary of it. Nor do I like its cheap and casual use within the religious community—"She's called to the fund-raising committee," "His call is to be an acolyte." But something certainly happened to me. A firm, insistent pressure between my shoulder blades was a felt presence, unnerving and unmistakable. Simone Weil called it "an impulse of an essentially and manifestly different order." She added, "Not to follow such an impulse . . . when it made itself felt, even if it demanded impossibilities, seemed to me the greatest of all ills."

Finally, I decided I needed what is called "spiritual direction." I had heard about spiritual directors from the others who attended Mass at the monastery; I wasn't sure what they were or what they did—psychoanalysis for the soul?—but I was willing to try.

I chose a woman priest close to my age whom I'd met a few times at the monastery. On the day I went to see her, she was seated in her office at the church she was working in at the time, a lovely redwood building two blocks from the Pacific Ocean. She had short, blond, no-nonsense hair and clear blue eyes. She wore a loosely gathered skirt, a red jacket, a black skirt, and a white collar. She greeted me and said, "Oh, I love your shoes, where did you get them?"

"Esprit," I said and thought, One more reason to ordain women as priests.

With great trepidation, I told her about the hand at my back. I was afraid, of course, that she would think I was crazy or overimaginative. If she had, I think my life would be very different now; at that stage everything was so new any skepticism would have felt like an assault. But as it happened, Anne Howard replied, matter-of-factly, "That's interesting. I felt it as someone pulling me."

This, then, is a record of what it is like to live with that hand at my back, to live within a world that is mostly unknown outside its boundaries, to live in faith. It's a long journey into experience and away from idealism. One imagines religion as making one "good," and various ideal ways of behaving are often touted in pulpits. But the opposite of sin is not virtue but faith. And none of it works without the weight of experience, knowing something as an experience rather than as an event that passes over the skin. How *this I* experiences *this event* and folds it into flesh. How a soul, as Margaret Drabble said, weathers into identity.

Faith is not about belief in something irrational or about a blind connection to something unreal. It's about a gathering, an accumulation of events and experiences of a different order.

These experiences are gradually convincing enough, or you have paid them so much attention, they reach critical mass. The famous "leap" comes at the beginning, when there is not enough experience to justify the effort. Even then, something begins faith—a memory of a reality or of an experience that doesn't quite fit with everything else, the longing a soul has to find its shape in the world.

Lent

LENT BEGINS ON Ash Wednesday, and as I walk into Trinity for the evening service, for the Litany of Repentance and the imposition of ashes, I'm in a haze of guilt, recrimination, and memories of giving up smoking. (Anne Howard says, "Anne's giving up drinking, Terri's giving up chocolate, and I'm just giving up.") It's early March and getting dark. Trinity is lit by old lanterns that hang from her ship's ceiling. The spare, flowerless altar is covered with a muslin cloth embroidered with a crown of thorns. Surrounded by rebuke, I hide in the shadows, try to look repentant, and listen to the sound of shoes slapping the tile floor, called the pavement, as my fellow sinners arrive. Within the Church at least, Lent's like Christmas: it's been overcommercialized. The "giving up" part is so dominant that what other meaning was there is eclipsed, hidden. And Lent's emphasis on sin and sacrifice is uncomfortable to me, as part of a generation determined to free itself from guilt. Churches have so often turned the word "sin" into an instrument of oppression and an assault on sexuality that it's hard to come by its meaning honestly. And yet today I have fasted—this and Good Friday being the only two formal fast days in the Episcopal Church—and arrived here, with an empty stomach and mixed motives, to try to sort things out.

The word "Lent" means "long spring days." It commemorates the forty days Jesus spent in the desert where he was led (or "driven," as some translations put it) shortly after his baptism, shortly after his epiphany. In the desert, he was "tempted by Satan." At Trinity, I think as I sit in my pew, we've been led or driven here tonight to have our foreheads smeared with ash.

We are going into Lent, someone said, as if Lent were something to fall into, a vessel. Victor Turner, the celebrated anthropologist, said that on a pilgrimage the whole of geography takes on symbolic meaning. We begin a pilgrimage on Ash Wednesday, a journey in which each step we take matches one in a story. It's like falling *into* a world, in which each movement reflects a movement elsewhere, each step is matched by another in a parallel dance.

The geography begins in the desert. In the crucible of heat and sand, Jesus was trying to figure out, as Frederick Buechner writes, "what it meant to be Jesus." In the weeks that follow Ash Wednesday, the Gospel readings recount what Jesus did afterward. He traveled: to a Samaritan city, Sychar, where a woman waited at a well; to a blind beggar's village; to Bethany, home of Martha and Mary's brother, Lazarus. He walked from town to town, sat down at the table with tax collectors and gluttons, talked to women, healed on the Sabbath, used the wrong fork. It is not at all clear to me that he knew who he was, as in "I'm the Son of God." Rather, it looks more like he discovered, step by step, more about himself as time wore on, as he walked, and waited, and healed.

At the end of Lent, on Palm Sunday, we walk with Jesus into Jerusalem, the city where crowds welcomed him on the Sabbath by spreading palm branches under his feet, and where he was executed on Friday.

"Ah Jerusalem, Jerusalem," Jesus cries in the Gospel of Luke. "The city that kills the prophets and stones those who are sent to it."

Lent is a journey toward the cross. And toward a tomb, and the mysterious, unending joy of those who found it empty.

The goal is to bring the journey's geography into the self, to bend beneath it, to allow the soul to find its narrative within it, its unfolding story. Lent is a journey that contains death, and death, as my therapist once said, cannot be simulated. On Ash Wednesday, I enter the desert. I become the woman at the well who demands, "Give me some of that water." I am the blind man begging for sight, the sisters of the dying brother, the halt and the lame calling out from the alleys and hedgerows, "Jesus, remember me," as the sweet song goes, "when you come into your kingdom."

Finally, on the eve of Easter, a priest lights the tall, white paschal candle in a darkened church. A deacon sings, "The light of Christ." It is a journey, as a biblical scholar put it, from ashes to fire.

ASH WEDNESDAY'S ASHES are made of palm fronds saved from Palm Sundays past and burned. In this first, ironic symbol of Lent, we are marked at the beginning of the journey with the scorched remains of its end. I found a small palm cross in the inside pocket of a purse I used four years ago, along with two tranquilizers and a glow-in-the-dark rosary. ("All bases covered," said Mark Benson.) That year I traveled frequently, researching magazine articles, and was overcome with anxiety at the moment of leaving home for each trip. In the spring of 1991, three days before I was to leave for Prague, I stood in line at a pharmacy craving Xanax like a junkie. I liked burning that past. I was both attracted and repelled by the thought that it would be "imposed" on me again, in a new configuration of atoms, as if my past could be rearranged and thus revisited.

Sam, our sexton, burned the palms with a little oil in a hibachi behind the church. Mark Asman put them in a pottery jar in the sacristy. They were dense, black, and soft as velvet.

. . .

AFTER BEN DIED, we scattered his ashes on the hillside above the monastery, behind a wooden cross. I had neither seen nor held the ashes of a person before. Ben's ashes were light gray and filled with bits of bone. When I held his urn, I was surprised by its weight: a small, dense package, like a newborn baby.

Shortly after Ben's service, I had a dream in which I crossed a series of borders into unknown territory. Waking, I desired to confess to someone, to God or to Ben, the things I had done and left undone while he lay dying.

Ann Jaqua and I drove up to the monastery to the cross where Ben's ashes were scattered. We sat down on the dry, sandy soil and made a circle of small stones. Then we each gathered up a handful of pebbles and began:

"This is for being afraid to kiss you, Ben," I said, dropping a pebble into the center of the cairn.

"This is for pretending I knew more than I did," said Ann.

"This is for washing my hands all the time."

"This is for wishing you would hurry up and die." By the end we had a sizable mound.

A hidden sense of having done wrong was like an irritant, a pebble in the shoe. I knew what was meant by a "grain" of truth. Making this "confession" might not make an immediate difference in my life or in Ann's life, but not making it—that is, not calling wrongdoing into consciousness—seemed to be fundamentally dangerous, leading to a kind of stupor. In a conversation a group of us had about evil, Betty Bickel said quietly, "What I know is that, little by little, it all adds up."

"I have come to call not the righteous," said Jesus, sitting down to dinner with Matthew, the tax collector, "but sinners."

. . .

PILGRIMS USED TO WALK the last mile of their journey barefoot. As I stand in line at Trinity with the others, awaiting the imposition of ashes, I see a path strewn with old shoes. The line moves forward and I kneel down on the old needlepoint cushions.

Martha Siegel imposes the ashes in a matter-of-fact, egalitarian style; she is careful not to show partiality, even to one sinner over another. I hear her steady voice as she walks down the line. She flicks my hair aside and makes the sign of the cross on my forehead. "Remember that you are dust," she says. "And to dust you shall return."

At first I feel the human touch, then embarrassment (What am I doing here?), then a quiet, communal shame. As we return from the altar, we try not to look at each other's foreheads. As I kneel down, I think about the temptations laid before Jesus in the desert. "Satan" put before him these three: If you are hungry, change stones into bread. If you are the Son of God, leap from a tower and rely on angels to rescue you. If you bow down before me, all the kingdoms of the world will be yours.

I suddenly see them, stories usually too archaic for my modern mind, as representing things all too familiar. Magical powers, helplessness, rescue, fame and power—they beckon me every day of my life. Just around the corner lies happiness; a new lover will provide lasting bliss; if I had what she has, then I would be . . .

They are the fantasies, the illusions, that suck out my vitality, that keep me from discovering my own rich reality. To come to terms with illusion is one of the great jobs of our lives: to discern what is fantasy and what is reality, what is dead and what is alive, what is a narcotic and what is food. It is dangerous, wrenching, and unavoidable. The seductive call of the Sirens was so compelling Odysseus lashed himself to his mast. In the desert, Jesus fought for his life.

What was asked of Jesus is what is asked of us: that we give up illusion—its false promises and its addicting inertia—and "come to our senses." That we, as Václav Havel would say, "live within the truth."

Later, Jesus would accomplish each one of these "temptations," but in a reversal of those days in the desert. He would change stones into bread: a few loaves of bread and five fish would feed five thousand. He would "hurl himself from a tower" and be "caught by angels," by giving up his life on the cross. He would be worshipped, by humbling himself as a servant.

If, instead of waiting for stones to be changed to bread, we share the food we have; if, rather than waiting for the fantasy job or lover, we take on the people and work of our lives; if, rather than waiting for rescue, we lay down our lives for our friends—then we depart the world of deadly illusion for a living reality in which "every day the real caress," as Anaïs Nin wrote, "replaces the ghostly lover."

As I sit in the shadowed church, I feel exhausted; some part of me just can't do it anymore. I'm not Jesus, after all, and I like my fantasies of power, love, and fame. Then I feel a sensation in my chest, near my heart. All at once I realize that I have been literally numb in that spot for years, and now I can feel there again. It's as if a tiny cellular area had been recalled to life. The place feels renewed, like a renovated room. It feels like falling *into* grace.

AFTER THE SERVICE I meet Chris Boesch in the parish hall. We have an appointment to talk to Ephraim, from the Kitchen. He's been panhandling again, he's shown up to work drunk twice, and last week he tried to break into the church. This is it; he's got to go. Chris meets me in the hall and says she's already talked to him; she met him on the street.

"I told him he had to get into a drug or alcohol program and only after that I would talk to him," she says. "He said I was the only person he could talk to. I said, In that case, you need to widen your circle. I've got to keep my boundaries."

I say something soothing, but I'm halfway out the door. I've got a dinner party to get to and I'm late. I think to myself, I'm glad I didn't talk to him; now it's not my problem.

TWO WEEKS AFTER Ash Wednesday, I attend a vestry meeting, having been elected in January to the body of lay-people who, with the priest, are responsible for running the parish. Until the sixties, almost half the Episcopal dioceses in the United States did not allow women to serve on vestries. Not until 1970 were women seated as deputies at the national Episcopal General Convention. In many churches there was no actual prohibition against women on a vestry because there was no need of one: almost no one imagined women in such places, least of all the women themselves. I once asked my mother why she stopped doing volunteer work for the church I was baptized in sometime in the late sixties, after I had gone away to college. She chewed on the question for a while, men-tioned the retirement of a priest she adored, how her work in a soup kitchen came to an end. Then her voice trailed off. "Maybe you hit the glass ceiling," I said. She gave no reply.

Trinity's vestry is made up of twelve people plus Mark Asman: six women and six men. We are each elected to a three-year term. We spent the weekend together in February, at a local retreat house run by conservative Episcopal nuns. The Sisters of the Holy Nativity do not recognize the ordina-tion of women. They do not allow women priests to preside at their altar. Six aging nuns are left in this house. That weekend, there were two male priests at the house: Mark and the rector from St. Patrick's in Thousand Oaks, south of Santa Barbara.

Each priest had a beautiful private room in the old part of the retreat center (the rest of us slept dormitory-style). If one of the priests spoke, six cowled heads turned simultaneously in his direction. The priests were unfailingly called "Father." In the first five hours we were there, I felt I had stumbled into an awful time warp, back to the prefeminist Church, but Mark's face took on a happy glow. I grew so irritated I took him aside in the garden before dinner and asked him how he'd feel if the nuns refused to allow an African-American priest to preside at the altar.

"They have good qualities," he answered.

"So do segregationists," I replied. As we entered the dining room together in unhappy silence, one of the sisters cried, "Oh, Father Asman."

The March vestry meeting's agenda reads as usual: "Guest Reports," "Treasurer's Report," "Capital Campaign" (we have to raise $1.5 million for the earthquake retrofit of the church). I look around the long library table at the people hunched over stacks of papers containing numbers. At the vestry retreat, we took the Myers Briggs Type Indicator Test, an interesting measure of personality traits and temperament that tends to help people understand how someone else can see things quite differently. We've derived benefits from the test already, chief among them that it's a great medium for jokes. Mark's "temperament" is "ISTJ": an introverted, sensing, thinking, judging type. His "temperament style"—supposedly "dutiful, serious, loyal, and industrious"—has provoked remarks about how boring Trinity is likely to become with such a one at the helm. I am kidded for being "sensitive, concerned with meaning, tend to wait until last minute to make decisions," the only "P" on the Myers Briggs scale: that is, the only "perceiving" personality. The rest of them are "J's," "judging" types. They like to make decisions. More than that may separate us. Until this year, I studiously kept to the margins at Trinity: working in the soup kitchen, planning alternative liturgies, sticking my toes in the water. Now here I am in the heart of the beast. Many of these people are, uh, Republicans.

Elly Wyatt, a beautiful woman with a halo of white hair, is the senior warden. A liberal Republican, she's a retired non-profit administrator. The junior warden is Kati Smith, who works as a fund-raiser for the local food bank. Our soup kitchen receives free groceries from them each week. Elaine Christ, the clerk of the vestry, a nurse at a local clinic, has a steadfast and original mind, and three dark-haired, intelligent children.

Stefani Schatz, one of the youngest vestry members at thirty-three, is a successful Mary Kay cosmetics saleswoman, who has recently begun the process of what the Church calls discerning a vocation to the Episcopal priesthood. Stephen Gibson is a partner in a funeral home, in his forties, the father of Nathan, born last year. Brian Meeder works with his partner, Jay Albert, in their sheet metal business. When they celebrated their tenth anniversary, I announced it in the newsletter and then battened down the hatches to await the reaction. There was no public reaction, which made me even more nervous. Betty Bickel runs her family's business: they make an instrument that measures light. She will be seventy this year. Betty has been at Trinity for thirty-five years. You can trace the history of women in the church by Betty's résumé: Sunday school teacher, Guild member, Stewardship Committee member, Outreach Committee chair, and, finally, vestry person. Ed Potts, a man in his fifties with a runner's lean build, is a vice president at Westmont College. He came to the Episcopal Church from another denomination two years ago. (He calls himself a "recovering Presbyterian." In recent years, many incoming Episcopalians have been from other Christian denominations.) Judy Brown grew up on her family's ranch near town. She has a solid head for finances. Michael Harris coordinates emergency services for Santa Barbara County. He and his wife, Lori, have a one-year-old boy and a five-year-old girl. Emmanual Itier, in his thirties, is an independent producer in the film business in Los Angeles.

Swimming through the financial reports, somewhat dizzy from numbers, we finally arrive at the slot on the agenda for the "Priest-in-Charge." It's Mark's turn for his report.

"I'd like us to go into executive session," says Elly Wyatt. I put down my pen. Mark clears his throat.

"There is something that is important to tell you," he says. "Members of the vestry who served last year already know this, but it's important to talk about it again, as a group, and to include all of you in the information." Here, he pauses. I notice that the senior and junior wardens are staring at their laps.

"I am a priest who also happens to be a gay man," he begins. His expression is that of a boy having to declare something hard and true. He taps his pen on his black church diary. A red ribbon marks the page. A beat of silence. I sneak a look at the people opposite me. They are impassive, except for Betty Bickel, who has tears in her eyes.

Mark clears his throat again. "This is part of who I am," he says. "It is not all of who I am, no more than anyone's sexuality is all of who they are. But it is an important part. And it has ramifications for you as a vestry, for me as a priest, and for Trinity as a faith community."

In 1979, the Episcopal Church at its National Convention narrowly passed an oddly worded resolution on human sexuality. After an introduction that stated, "homosexual persons are children of God," it *recommended* that bishops and other persons responsible for approving candidates for ordination *consider* the candidates' marital status and sexual chastity. Its last line reads, "Therefore, we believe it is not appropriate for this Church to ordain a practicing homosexual, or any person who

is engaged in heterosexual relations outside of marriage."
In the sixteen years since the resolution passed, liberal and conservative bishops have volleyed as to whether it carried the
force of law or "doctrine," or what the word "recommend"
actually means. In 1994 fifty-five bishops signed the Koinonia
Statement ("koinonia" means "sharing or fellowship"). In part,
it read

> We believe that sex is a gift from God . . . that some of us
> are created heterosexual and some of us are created
> homosexual . . . that both homosexuality and heterosex-
> uality are morally neutral, that both can be lived out
> with beauty, honor, holiness and integrity.
>   . . . we believe that gay or lesbian persons who do
> not chose to live alone, but forge relationships of their
> choice that are faithful, monogamous, committed, life-
> giving and holy are to be honored.
>   We also believe that the ordained ranks of the church
> are open to all baptized Christians.

Since 1979, bishops have continued to ordain gay men and
lesbian women as deacons and priests, but many of those
ordained have remained either closeted or celibate or both. In
1990, however, Walter Righter, an assisting bishop in Newark,
New Jersey, ordained a male deacon, Barry Stopfel, who was
openly living with another man. A year later, Stopfel was
ordained to the priesthood by Bishop John Shelby Spong of
the same diocese. Rumors are floating this spring that a group
of conservative bishops are going to attack Bishop Righter—
to "present" him for heresy before an ecclesiastical court. This
possibility is seen as not only a legal maneuver, but a political
one: it could have a chilling effect on bishops like Righter and
prevent what conservatives see as a replay of the "irregular"
ordinations of women and the "regularizing" that immediately

followed them. I asked George Barrett, our retired bishop, a few weeks ago if he thought the conservatives would succeed. He replied that they simply didn't have the numbers—a presentment must be signed by at least seventy-five of the church's two hundred and ninety-seven bishops.

Because the issue has not been resolved at the higher levels of the church, the parish level is left in both confusion and a kind of freelance freedom. No one knows exactly what the national church will or will not legally allow, and so each diocese more or less decides for itself what the "atmosphere" around homosexual priests will be. Each parish then takes its cue from its own diocese. All this is covert; the process itself is in the closet. The Diocese of Los Angeles, for example, is headed by three liberal bishops, all of whom signed the Koinonia Statement. Gay and lesbian priests in L.A. feel relatively free, although not all of them are open to their parishes.

In the Diocese of San Joaquin in central California, things are completely reversed. Bishop John-David Schofield is openly opposed to noncelibate homosexual priests. He believes that "physical sexual expression is appropriate only within the lifelong monogamous union of husband and wife." The ordination of noncelibate homosexual persons, Bishop Schofield believes, "deviates and departs from the biblical norm." If there are any homosexual priests in his diocese, they are closeted.

At the vestry meeting, Mark continues: "Because we are in the process of deciding whether or not I will be called as your rector, we will need to take this into consideration." He wants volunteers, he says, for a committee that will work on a way we can talk together "about this issue" as a vestry. Several people raise their hands.

"If that's all," the senior warden says, "we'll go out of executive session."

Betty Bickel raises her hand. "That couldn't have been easy for you, Mark. I'd like to honor your courage." We applaud and he smiles shyly, tapping his black shoe against the leg of the table.

As we march back into the agenda, I wonder how this is sitting with the more conservative members of the vestry. Do they care? If they do, will they find a place to express it? But right now, the Worship Council wants to talk about Holy Week; Parish Life and Growth needs more people to donate money for altar flowers; Education's April adult forum isn't working out.

It's late when the meeting adjourns, but a few of us linger on the sidewalk. We seem to have nothing to say, and yet we can't leave. Finally, Mark comes out and we cluster around him—like chickens, I think later, under the wing of a hen. Or like bodyguards.

Later in the week, I ask Mark if I might hear the whole story. He agrees, and we sit in the library at Trinity talking for several hours.

"When I was a young priest I was quite conservative," Mark begins. "I believed that homosexuality was something one had to struggle to control and overcome. So much energy went into fighting my sexuality that my world was highly compartmentalized and disconnected. I believed that homosexual priests had to be celibate. I was against the ordination of women. I was conservative in my interpretation of scripture— an evangelical, not a fundamentalist. That world says there is an Evil One and you had to fight him. The image I had of God was a sort of divine Santa Claus. I had an idealized notion of who I was and was meant to be, a narrow view of grace, and an institutional view of the church. My mentor was David Schofield, my priest, who later became the Bishop of San Joaquin.

"In June of 1975, I was ordained to the deaconate and hired at a parish in Santa Cruz. In five months, in October, the rector announced his retirement. I was ordained to the priesthood in January, at the age of twenty-five, and found myself priest-in-charge of a parish of eight hundred members.

"For a year, I served as priest-in-charge. Then the parish hired a new rector. [The Episcopal Church usually does not allow a priest-in-charge of a parish to become its rector.] I served as the new rector's curate. This arrangement rarely works out, and it didn't in my case. I began looking for another job in late 1977. In June of 1978, I was called to a church in Oroville, in northern California, where I worked for four years.

"When I was in Santa Cruz, I had met with a woman who did healing prayer, regarding my sexuality. I got to the point where I thought I was healed, so to speak. While I was in Oroville, I met a woman, in December of 1978, and we started dating and got engaged. But the engagement ended and as a result, my homosexuality came raging back. In desperation, I sought help from the woman who had prayed with me before in Santa Cruz, and from David Schofield. I was ready to leave parish ministry, to try to come to terms with myself, but David asked me to try exorcism before I did that. I did try exorcism, in the summer of '81, but it didn't 'work.' I finally realized that my whole world was unraveling, that nothing I had done was working, that I was becoming depressed and negative, and the only alternative was to leave parish ministry and find a way to accept my sexuality. I couldn't see how to deal with it in a small parish in a conservative town. I spent the next year organizing the parish and my life to leave as quietly and thoughtfully as possible in order not to burn any bridges. I left in '82, with the blessings of the parish and my bishop."

Mark takes a sip of coffee. "I moved in with my father and stepmother in Inverness. I thought that if I was ever to have a real relationship with my father, I would have to tell him, so I did. He was very supportive and understanding. He said, 'I want to cry for myself, because I'll never have grandchildren that will bear my name. And I want to cry for you because of all you've had to carry alone.'

"I had saved some money and with a gift from the parish, I had enough to live on for six months. After six months, it became clear to me that I needed more time, and I began looking for a job. I went to work for I. Magnin as Christmas help and I also worked as an evening telephone solicitor for the March of Dimes. I rented a room in the Castro district [San Francisco's gay neighborhood] from a close friend. I began to discover what living was like with all of me available to myself.

"For the first time in my life, I wasn't going to church. It was a year and a half before I did. I had tremendous contempt for the institution. I didn't know how to relate to it. But even though I was estranged from the Church, my priesthood was still intact. I had no crisis with my connection to God. Everything else, however, was up for grabs.

"Finally, in the spring of 1984, I ran into a good friend from college who turned out to be gay. He was Roman Catholic and part of Dignity [the organization for gay Roman Catholics]. He and I went to a workshop at a storefront in the Castro sponsored by the Episcopal Diocese of California and taught by a priest entitled 'How to Come Out.' It was the beginning of Lent.

"I began attending services at the Church of the Advent. I sat in the pew for six months, then I transferred my license from the Diocese of Northern California to the Diocese of California and began working as a volunteer assisting priest.

"I hadn't figured out how to relate to the larger Church. The Church of the Advent was mostly gay; we were in the gay ghetto of the Church. I was learning how to be with other gay people, on my own, but I was not confronting the larger Church.

"The shift in my theology was incremental. I did realize

early on that if I was going to be free, everyone had to be free. I could no longer hold women hostage. They had as much right to be priests as I did.

"I thought I would stay at I. Magnin for a couple of years. It turned into ten. I was quite happy working for I. Magnin. I worked in sales, and then moved up the ladder to general manager. In 1990, I moved to Chicago, where I stayed two years. During those years, I thought about going back into parish ministry full-time, but I didn't feel quite ready. I needed to have time to live more freely. I knew that sometime my priesthood would become my vocation again. In the meantime, it was good to work outside the church. I became more confident as I made my way in the world. Then, in April of 1992, I was transferred to Los Angeles.

"I began to realize that my career with I. Magnin had played itself out. The company was in Chapter 11. All of the signs told me this was the time to leave. I met with the staff person in charge of clergy deployment in the Diocese of Los Angeles. He and I talked about how a good way to make the transition to full-time ministry would be through an interim position. I told him he needed to know that I was a priest who happened to be gay, that I had respect for the priesthood and the Church, but I was not going to go back into the closet for parish ministry.

"When the Trinity job came up, I talked to Anne Howard, in her capacity as the canon to the ordinary, about whether to disclose my sexuality to the search committee. She didn't think it was necessary. One of the differences between being called as a rector and as an interim is that in the case of a rector, the focus is much more on the person. In the case of an interim, the focus is more on the parish. I told her that at the same time, I wasn't going to hide my sexuality. I was going to live my life as honestly and as sensitively as I knew how.

"When the diocese and the vestry asked me to consider a new arrangement at Trinity, in August last year, then I realized I had to more clearly define myself for the parish. I began preaching more assertively, about my stance on justice and other issues. And I knew that at some point I would have to disclose myself to the full vestry."

When Mark finishes speaking, I feel disoriented and depressed. Then I feel rage. Injustice has a price: it exacts itself in a specific human history, specific flesh.

THIS LENT, I work in the Community Kitchen, every day, starting at noon. The weather has been alternately rainy and sunny and warm. When it's sunny, the men like to sit on the grass outside the church or on the steps leading into the parish hall. But they can't, according to the Kitchen's new agreement with Trinity. That's why I'm here—to be the monitor, as we described it in a committee meeting; to be the enforcer, as I put it to myself. Day after day, I walk around the grounds with my little name tag ("Hi, my name is Nora") and bump guys off the lawn. "Excuse me," I say to two men, one of whom is sitting on a piece of cardboard, the other on a bright Hawaiian shirt. They are leaning against the church wall sunning themselves. "You are welcome to sit over on those benches." I gesture to the back door of the church, where the entrance to the Kitchen is. "But not here." If I run into resistance, I say weakly, "We have little old lady parishioners. And they need to be able to use these steps." This is the truth, but we all know that it's only part of the truth. The other part of the truth is that the little old lady parishioners, and other parishioners as well, don't like the sight of these men—dirty, ragged, smelly—on those steps. (Friday morning at the monastery, Nick Radelmiller, one of the monks, gave a homily in which he quoted from a book of letters written by a Roman Catholic priest dying of AIDS. He had found a certain peace in the stark realities of his illness, he wrote, because in normal life "we drown in half-truths.")

I am here, on the lawn, drowning in half-truths. A few days ago, I asked a man to leave the front steps of the parish hall, near the office.

"You may sit over there, on the benches," I said.

"That's a good thing," he replied, "because I need thirty-five thousand dollars for brain surgery."

One of the men near us asked me what my job was at the church and I replied that I was "the liaison to the Community Kitchen from the church."

"And this is part of your job?" he asked, gesturing toward the steps.

"Yes," I replied.

He seemed satisfied that being an enforcer was part of my job description. I might be an asshole, but at least I wasn't a gratuitous asshole.

Last week, I saw a young man and woman sitting on the steps of the church, their bicycles near them, leaning against the railing, eating takeout sandwiches from Cantwell's, the store across the street. I decided not to bounce them. Then they were joined by a homeless guy, right out of the Kitchen, with long hair, ragged clothes, and bare feet. The Holy Spirit had just upped the ante. I couldn't bounce him and not them. As I thought about it, I realized I couldn't bounce anyone from the steps of the church, any more than I could bounce someone from inside it.

Earlier this week, I was sitting upstairs with a couple of people planning a service when Rachel, the church secretary, buzzed me. The owner of Cantwell's wanted to talk. I picked up the phone and Joe Atwill said that two guys "from the Kitchen" had been caught shoplifting the day before; when one of his checkers tried to stop them, he was assaulted.

"I don't know what to do," he said. "This is the third incident that's drawn blood. We want to support you, but can't you
monitor them better?"

"I'm sorry about this, Joe," I replied.

"Can't you bus them in and then bus them back downtown?"

"I don't think so."

"A lot of businesspeople in the area are upset about this."

I suggested a meeting the next day with Joe, the other
businesspeople, John Richards, the chair of the Kitchen's steering committee, and me.

When I returned to the church that afternoon, Mike, the
Kitchen's janitor, stopped me as I was getting out of my car.

"Can I talk to you?" he asked.

"Sure."

"I think that Cody has AIDS," he said. "So do a lot of other
guys. He's been handling food."

I explained that you can't catch AIDS from someone's
hands, but Mike didn't look satisfied. We have made a rule in
the Kitchen that someone who is ill can't handle the food, and
I wondered what I was going to do with this one. When I got
inside the church, Sam took me aside and said, "I guess I'd better tell you about this before anyone else does. There was an
incident today. A guy was leaning over the fence looking at the
children and a teacher told him not to and he began yelling
obscenities at her."

I studied his face. Often, when Sam tells me something bad
about the Kitchen, he has a kind of triumphant "I told you
so" look that makes me scream inside. I am never sure with
Sam just which side he's on. It seems to me he takes pleasure in
incidents in which the Kitchen comes up short, especially
those in which he proves that I'm a Bleeding Heart Liberal.
Then he turns around and mothers Faustino and some of the
other men who work in the Kitchen, cooking for them and
making it easy for them to sleep on the porch. He's young—

twenty-five—and arrived at Trinity last year from New York, where he used to cook for an AIDS project. He's a real chef, everything he cooks is delicious, and he plays the oboe beautifully to boot.

My relationship with Sam is often awkward. The sexton at any church is the lowest person on the totem pole and he is likely to compensate by being ornery and hard to please. For my part, I feel intimidated by him. He's so young and male, and I believe he thinks I'm a weak woman. I want to prove to him how strong I am. We bump against each other, our defensive postures intact. Every now and then, however, one of us will let down his or her guard. Early in the days of the Thursday Night Eucharist, Martha Siegel and I forgot to buy bread for the service one night and ended up using a loaf of French bread out of the pantry with pesto, sun-dried tomatoes, and olives in it as Eucharist bread. Sam, who doesn't go to church now but was raised in an Episcopal household, was so horrified he offered to bake Eucharist bread for us for all eternity and has done so ever since.

Sam's face as he told me about this latest incident in the Kitchen remained impassive. I decided to take him at his word, and thanked him for telling me right away.

John Richards met with Joe at Cantwell's and I tracked down the principal of the Montessori school, Jim Fitzpatrick, who was leading the children back from the park next door.

"I'm not sure what happened," Jim said to me, "but I think that one of the teachers—a new teacher, on whom we've impressed the need to put the care of the children first—saw a man leering, as she put it, over the back fence at the kids."

"Which fence?" I asked.

"The one near the parking lot," Jim replied. "I think that the man was standing up on top of something so he could see over the fence. I guess the guy started screaming at her and she went looking for someone to help from the Kitchen."

We talked some more and it came down to the same line that Joe at Cantwell's used: Can't they just go somewhere else?

"But where?" John had said to Joe.

"How about down by the railroad tracks?" Joe had said.

"The tourists are down there," John replied. "The tourists don't like them."

"How about a place where there aren't professional women around it?" said Joe, adding, "My clientele. Or the school. I think it's not good to have the Kitchen so close to a school."

"But there isn't a place in Santa Barbara," John replied, "where there isn't some kind of business or professional building. Do you think we shouldn't have the Kitchen at all?"

"No," said Joe. "I'm in favor of the Kitchen. I know you guys are doing good work. It's just hard on us. It's so hard on us."

They had reached this impasse, John reported to me, and shaken hands.

What we want is for them to disappear, I thought. God knows, sometimes I do. I'm sick of the man leering over the fence. (But was he actually "leering"? I wonder. Could he have only been watching the children?) Sick of the men on the lawn, sick of the men who scream at me, "Fuck off, fuck off, fuck off!" when I ask them to move to the benches.

Did Jesus get sick of the prostitutes, the halt, the blind, the lame, the lepers, the tax collectors? Does Jesus get sick of me?

Then yesterday, as I was wiping down trays, I turned and in the turning, the room changed the same way it had during Advent. The room filled up. I was swimming, but it was like swimming in sunlight or honey. A homeless woman, Marilyn, who dresses wonderfully—today in a flowered hat and long blue silk dress over another dress—was sitting at a table, laughing.

"I work here," Mark Benson said, "because I must."

Today, I find a lock has been put on the door to the laundry and shower room. No one seems to know who put it there. When I ask Mark Asman about it, he says he didn't know the lock was there, but someone found Faustino cooking for his friends one Sunday morning and didn't like it. "Someone" has complained that the men who work in the Kitchen were doing their laundry.

"That's one of the ways we 'pay' them," I reply. "They work in the Kitchen every day for free."

"I think it may be too much. Asking too much."

"The Kitchen pays for half the utilities."

"I know," he replies, then continues: "Even All Saints in Pasadena—a parish we all revere for its liberal views—had to move its homeless program off the church grounds."

He gets up and goes into his office. He returns with a postcard.

"I got this yesterday," he says, handing it to me. "I haven't shown it to anyone else, nor do I intend to."

I read, "I hate what you're doing to this part of town. I have to pass homeless men who urinate in the bushes and they hassle older people. You are enabling alcoholics and I want you to stop."

WE STUMBLE THROUGH LENT. I shout at Vincent, he shouts back.

"Too bad your religion doesn't give you a better nature!" he yells. Too bad, indeed. It doesn't seem to have done a thing for my nature.

"I wish I were a better person," I say to Ed Potts. He replies, "God isn't interested in getting righteous people into heaven, but in developing souls."

One afternoon, as another storm is brewing, I go for tea with Elizabeth Corrigan, Dan Corrigan's wife. She is ninety-three. She greets me at the door.

"The wind just blew down my awning," she says happily.

"Where is it?" I ask.

"In my neighbor's yard," she replies. "Let's have a glass of wine."

Elizabeth and I sit in her living room, drinking cheap white wine, eating shortbread, and watching the wind blow the palm trees horizontal. As the evening descends, the rain is coming down in sheets, and great patches of darkness spread across the city, interspersed with areas of light. The power is out. I wonder if I can cross Mission Creek to get home. But I am happy here with Elizabeth, getting buzzed.

"A few days after Dan and I were married," she says, "we went on our honeymoon. We had no money at all, but one of his parishioners had lent us his cabin. It was on an island in a lake in northern Minnesota. We went up there and on the way, Dan wanted to stop at a little church to check on it. A deacon was there; they had no priest. He asked Dan if he would come back the following Sunday to say Mass. They hadn't had a priest, or a Eucharist, in weeks. Dan looked at me and I frowned. That Sunday would be the last day of our honeymoon. But he said yes. As we got in the car, he said to me, 'They need the Eucharist and besides, we'll get a good meal from the deacon if we come down Saturday night.'

"The next Saturday, we rowed across the lake and got in the car and drove down to the little church. I was looking forward to a real home-cooked meal. When we got to the deacon's house, there was a note on the door: he had taken the opportunity to go to New York. Inside the house, there was no food. Just a bag of peanuts. I sat down and ate the peanuts and cried. I was beginning to get a sense of what it was like to be married to a priest."

Dan died on their sixty-eighth wedding anniversary, September 21, last fall. A few hours before his death, he told Elizabeth, "What a wonderful life we've had together."

At Dan's funeral, his old friend Basil Meeking, Roman Catholic Bishop of Christchurch, New Zealand, said of him, "Above all, Daniel Corrigan was set free by hope."

Elizabeth takes a sip of wine and says to me, "After Dan died, I put a picture of him near my crucifix. When I prayed in the morning, I would look at his picture. A couple of days ago, I was praying and I realized I was looking at Dan the whole time. I said, 'Darling, I've been praying to you all this time. Now it's time I prayed to Him.' "

AT THE THURSDAY evening Eucharist late in Lent, we ask at the beginning of the service, "Who have I hurt this week?" And then, "Who has hurt me?"

Anne Howard, just returned from her commute to the Diocese in Los Angeles, preaches. "It is the allegiance we form that tells the tale. What have I lost in order to achieve influence, a sense of my own importance? What relationships suffer because I choose to do such a good, such powerful good, even good under the artful guise of humble service to the Church?"

Earlier in the week, she and I met for spiritual direction at the Red Lion Inn, a huge hotel near the beach. We stopped by her car in the parking lot so she could pick up her mobile phone "in case the bishop needs me."

As we swam through the gargantuan lobby of the hotel, Anne said she'd been thinking about our covenant relationship with God, "a covenant built on promises, faith, and response."

I was struck by our incongruity: in this vast lobby, surrounded by people who were pretending they were in Palm Springs, Anne with the telephone in the pocket of her jacket linked to Los Angeles, where the diocese answers with a recording ("You have reached the Episcopal Diocese of Los Angeles. If you know the extension . . ."), talking about God's covenant. We were on an island, a finger of land, and all around us lapped the waters of wall-to-wall carpets, sound-proofing, people in golf clothes, and the church's institutional identity.

"How does that covenant take place?" Anne asked, as we crossed the boulevard to the beach. "And what tempts us away from it? Not the usual temptations, like sleeping with someone other than your husband or eating too much chocolate cake, but what distracts us from the covenant?"

CARRIE BROTHERS IS at the service tonight. She's huge with child; the baby is due right after Easter. She wears her waist-length hair braided down her back. When we exchange the Peace, I hug Carrie and pat her braid. It feels like a rope.

Lois Hitz stands next to Carrie. Elegant in heavy silk pants and a white T-shirt, she's thin all over except for her belly, which is bloated. On her right wrist are two silver bracelets, one with a tawny stone. Last week, she taught a section of Trinity's Lenten series, "Whole and Forgiven," on the Good Samaritan.

At the base community this evening, she says, "There's always that blank space between praying to have the courage to do something and then doing it."

"I like you guys," says Mark Benson. "I like it that we can sit in silence for two or three minutes and not get nervous."

In the guild hall nearby, Grey Brothers is leading the choir in practice. They are singing "Domine deus, filius patris, miserere nobis." God the Father, God the Son, have mercy on us.

My brother, Kit, is well enough to go back to work, and he and I are rejoicing. He's surveying the Rio Grande in New Mexico for the Bureau of Land Management, from as far north as Espanola above Santa Fe, to Truth or Consequences, south of Socorro. Standing on a bluff over Otowi Bridge on the highway to Los Alamos, he sights through his instrument across the river, to a second point miles away. When I listen to him describe his work, I think that he is connecting points all across New Mexico, making sense of geography.

Out in the field, he marches through salt cedar, cactus, willows—the bosque, as it is called in New Mexico, a generic term for impenetrable brush. Once he was walking with his crew early in the morning near the river. Huge spiderwebs covered in dew just over his head absorbed him so much he didn't look where he was going. The rattle woke him up; his boot landed inches from a fat snake, coiling to strike. "I try not to kill them," he told me. "Bad karma."

On the phone one evening, Kit told me he's had a fight with Rande, his wife. "About this midlife crisis," he said, "when does it end?"

Tonight, we read the story of the Prodigal Son. We all know the story: A father has two sons. One of them stays on the farm. The other takes his inheritance, squanders it, and ends up living among the pigs and their food—pea pods, in some translations. One morning he gets up and can't stand it anymore. He turns toward home.

The boy stands before his father. He says, "Father, I have sinned." His father embraces him and throws a party.

Mark Benson asks, "What does it mean—the squandering of his inheritance?"

"Lately I've been thinking about it as self-betrayal," Ann Jaqua replies. "The boy squandered his true self, all of the best that was in him."

I sit at the base community listening to the choir singing, and I think, Have mercy on us. Help us to discard all those things that keep us from our true self, everything that squanders our inheritance, the dust in our mouths, what gets in the way. Help us rise from the ashes. Bring us through the desert. In the midst of it, remind us that it isn't done by "giving things up for Lent," or by playing by the rules.

After Constantine, emperor of Rome, converted to Christianity, and the Church stopped being a small, illegal sect and became a state religion, various Christian men moved into the desert, often into Egypt, to live simpler lives and to counteract what they saw as a dangerous affiliation with power. The Desert Fathers, as they came to be called, hoped to become truly pure, to escape temptation and experience the holy as directly as was possible. They fasted and prayed and welcomed strangers. Out of them came what are now the monastic orders.

One of the stories about them concerns two monks, a young one and an elder.

"Abbot Lot came to Abbot Joseph and said, 'Father, according as I am able, I keep my little rule, and my little fast, my prayer, my meditation and contemplative silence, and according as I am able, I strive to cleanse my heart of thoughts. Now what more should I do?'

"The elder rose up in reply and stretched out his hands to heaven and his fingers became like ten lamps. . . . He said, 'Why not be totally changed into fire?' "

Holy Week

MY FIRST MAUNDY THURSDAY service was spent at the monastery two years ago, after Robert Hagler had arrived as the new prior. A thin, graying priest in his forties who wears polo shirts and khakis, Robert likes to stand outside Mount Calvary's front door, look down at the Pacific, and smoke. One Friday morning when traffic was getting a little thick for the seven-thirty Mass, Robert took a last puff and asked me to direct the cars. "I have to go in and put on some socks before I celebrate," he said, looking down at his moccasined feet. "When we reformed the Church, we got rid of the altar slippers, but we kept the socks."

On Maundy Thursday the Church begins the Triduum, the Three Days, which last from the evening of Maundy Thursday to vespers on Easter Day. The Triduum is the hinge between Lent and Easter, between the guilt and shame of Lent, the inertia and fear that bind us to the past and leave us in despair, and the love that lures us toward hope. The three days are like time out of time. Each day is packed with services, usually two to a day, and each service is packed with liturgy, some of it dating back to the second century.

"Liturgy" means, literally, "the people's work" and is the name put to ordered, communal worship. Annie Dillard writes in *Holy the Firm* that she often thinks of "the set pieces of liturgy as certain words which people have successfully addressed to God without their getting killed."

Think of a liturgy as a Native American corn dance. Such a ritual is not "merely superstitious"—that is, not a matter of "If we dance these steps correctly, the rain will come." It is, instead, connective tissue between muscle and bone, that which binds us to a Word, a reality blazing behind the curtain of daily life.

"For a people to do their liturgy, they must have done something else," writes Gabe Huck, a Roman Catholic priest. "For a people to do the vigiling and the renouncing and the promising and the baptizing and the Eucharist, they must come hungry, famished, for God's word, for the deeds they do in community, for the water and for the bread and the wine."

The "Maundy" in Maundy Thursday comes from "mandatum," the mandate: "You must love one another." As the Gospels tell it, Jesus and his friends were in the upper room of what may have been an inn, just inside Jerusalem's walls, eating a Passover Seder. During supper, Jesus "rose from the table, laid aside his garments, and taking a towel, tied it round him. Then he poured water into a basin, and began to wash his disciples' feet and to wipe them with a towel. When it was Simon Peter's turn, Peter said to him, 'You, Lord, washing my feet?' Jesus replied, 'You do not understand now what I am doing, but one day you will.' "

Robert had planned that evening's liturgy for several weeks. He studied a text devoted to the Triduum written by a Roman Catholic priest, ironed the altar linen, and washed two tall glasses he bought on sale at Crate & Barrel to use as chalices. He said he'd been thinking about "water, feet, towels, and Jesus."

As the service began, we filed in, maybe forty of us, and sat down in the dark wood pews. My college friend Ellin and her daughter, Jamie, had come down from the Bay Area for a visit.

Jamie was then nine, a skinny colt with a cloud of wavy dark hair. She was wearing a black-and-white-checked dress with a spray of bright red fake cherries at the throat that she'd ordered herself from a catalog.

Next to Ellin were a quiet nun, and Ben. Ben's doctors had just begun feeding him intravenously. On his back he wore a gray-and-blue backpack in which there was a plastic bag of nutrients and a pump that made a wheezing noise every few seconds. Ben called it the Holy Tit.

Robert had dimmed the lights in the chapel. Two candles were lit on the altar and, across the room, a tall wrought-iron candelabra stood on either side of a low bench.

After the homily, two of the monks brought out a large oval basin, two pitchers of water, and two stacks of white towels. They placed them in front of the bench. Robert invited us to stand and make two lines in front of the pews.

Because of the silence and the nearly dark room, I felt as if I were moving into an intimacy, a kind of embrace. While waiting in line, you could not easily guess whose feet you'd be washing or who would be washing yours. Robert said, "You might look at the person whose feet you are washing as the Christ."

The nun washed Ellin's feet with dispatch, didn't raise her eyes to Ellin's face, put the cloth down, and returned quickly to her pew. (I wondered how she'd look at Christ. With dispatch?)

Then it was Ellin's turn to wash. She knelt beside the basin, and Jamie took the seat. She extended her long foot and her mother took it into her hand, poured the water over it—you could hear the sound of the water falling into the pan—her eyes were on her daughter's face. Ellin kissed Jamie's foot so gently it was like a sigh.

When it was my turn, I knelt down, looked up, and saw Ben. The "Holy Tit" made its frightening wheeze. I poured water over his foot while holding it in my hand. His foot was lean and brown. I held it so carefully as I was drying it that I realized I was trying to hold on to his life. Still holding his foot in the towel, I leaned down to kiss it. Then, I looked up at him; he looked down at me. I saw in him not the best that was in him, but what made him uniquely Ben, what made him not any other person in the world: his memories, his imagination, his tenderness, and his hope. And I saw something else, Good Friday's shadow, way in the back of his eyes.

THIS YEAR HOLY WEEK falls in early April, between April Fool's and tax day, a coincidence I'm sure the Holy Spirit finds amusing. St. Paul said we should be fools for Christ, and I am foolish this year. The big winter storms have rearranged the landscape; whole cliffs have fallen down, leaving rubble on well-known hiking trails, and have transformed our creeks into rivers. One storm dumped six inches in an hour, flooded the parish hall at Trinity, and nearly drowned the library. Landscape is sacramental, to be read as text, said the poet Seamus Heaney; this year the Holy Week landscape is a deconstruction, a disassembling, and, of course, a cleansing, a washing away. At a planning session for the Holy Week liturgy, Chris Boesch announced she thought the theme of the week should be water.

The church calendar is fixed, although it doesn't stand apart from the rhythm of time. Every year, Easter follows the first full moon after the spring equinox. In my Day-Timer meetings are never certain until they actually happen; we all seem to be looking over each other's shoulders for greener grass. Into this free fall, I welcome the unalterable calendar. I pour myself into planning Holy Week liturgies. I dream of sitting inside an earthenware vessel.

"What if the vessel fills up?" asks Anne Howard.

"I would drown," I reply.

She grins. "What if it filled up with light?"

ON MAUNDY THURSDAY, I arrive at Trinity at noon to work in the soup kitchen. St. John Chrysostom said that there is a liturgy after the liturgy, that work in the world is inseparable from worship. Here, today, the Kitchen feels like worship itself; the altar table in the nearby sanctuary has meaning only because of this table, full of day-old bread and grapefruit salad.

Karen Torjesen, in her book *When Women Were Priests*, describes "house churches," which were the meeting places for the early Christians. Torjesen believes the early church was "informal, often countercultural in tone, and was marked by a fluidity and flexibility that allowed women, slaves and artisans to assume leadership roles." Because Christians thought of themselves as "an alternative family" and often met in homes, women assumed leadership within the church, "teaching, disciplining, nurturing and administrating."

Maybe the Kitchen is like one of those early churches where everyone was welcome—or, at least, women, slaves, and artisans were welcome, those people who didn't have authority or even personhood in public life. Here we may be recreating the original Eucharist, a feast for the marginal, while there, in the church, is its reified progeny. A conservative priest from Slovakia once visited the Kitchen and asked me why we didn't have a prayer before lunch. "The lunch is the prayer," I said, surprised at myself.

Just as I begin serving, a young man appears, walking in a bike that is packed with plastic bags. As he nears the table, I can see that each bag has some small item in it, bound inside the bag. The overall effect is of little nodules covering his bike, as if his bike were growing small plastic plants. He says as he picks up his plate that he's discovered he can pour vinegar in his ears for a recurring ear infection. Better, he says, than what his doctors recommend. As he leaves that day, he says to me, "I've figured out what I'm running from."

"What is that?" I ask.

"From the winter," he replies. "From the heavy dew in the mornings and the cold at night."

He pauses. "And from the aging process. And from time."

Then he adds, "And, of course, my mother."

As the Kitchen stops serving, Mike begins cleaning the floor. He told me earlier that he may have found a full-time job, although it sounds a bit vague. "I just can't make it on what I make here," he said, "and I have to make my child support. Get off the streets." He was speaking very fast, faster than usual, and as he spoke, his eyes scanned the room; he never looked at me. I noticed that he'd lost weight. His potbelly was gone. I couldn't tell whether he was negotiating for a higher salary and more hours, telling me the truth, or both. I had nothing more to offer him and I told him so. Always before I'd felt comfortable in Mike's presence, but as I left him, I felt uneasy.

As soon as the Kitchen guests have left, Sam and I make a U shape with twelve tables, and I begin covering them with white sheets of varying sizes. Betty Bickel has ironed them all at home. Pat, an elderly woman with years of service at Trinity, walks out to see what I'm up to. She took me aside earlier to tell me she had a vision in the morning service. I felt caught between wanting just to soothe her and please her ("Nice, Pat") and wanting to make sure that in this realm, at least, I would have some integrity. But as she told me about it—"I was praying and I suddenly felt Jesus standing next to me and I felt a peace"—I had a feeling of calm, a rush of holy sweetness, and I believed her.

Now, as if to reinforce the authenticity of her claim, she

doesn't ask me what I'm doing, as she has in the past, but says instead, "What can I do to help you?" She offers to set the tables, a Godsend, literally.

I go outside to search for buckets for the foot washing and find a white one, turned upside-down, in the children's play yard. I pick it up, then see in front of me a series of items: an old toy stove, a washcloth, a bowl. For a second they remain disconnected; then I see what unifies them. Faustino, the Kitchen cook, lives outside and sleeps on the church porch. This is where he washes up in the morning and evening. It's his dressing room, disguised by what I see and what I don't see, by the curtain between me and reality. The bucket is his chair. I put it back.

Back inside the parish hall, I adjust the sheets. On the tables I place white cyclamen in pots, and votive candles in what are called shot glass holders, a name I cherish in this setting. Betty will come in around four after work, to finish decorating.

As I move more and more into the center of church activity, I often associate church not with God or peace, but with lists. Holy Week is the ultimate list. Scrawled on my Palm Sunday bulletin are the words "Dodie, eight buckets, pitchers, pails, bowls." We've made the decision this year to have the service in the parish hall rather than the church for the first time. We've gone back and forth on this decision: it will be more informal in the parish hall, more like a meal, yet we are breaking with tradition, always a dangerous move in a church. "Towels, wafers, candles, bunches of rosemary, rent two 8′ × 3′ tables, purificator, corporal, flashlights . . ." All of us are frayed by ambivalence and ready to fix blame.

Chatting with Scott Richardson, the rector of St. Mary's Episcopal Church in nearby Lompoc, I said, "You know, I find myself cracking the whip over all the volunteers I've been working with on this service. That isn't right for church work."

"That's true," he said. "Although there is a lot of whip-cracking in the New Testament. Jesus does some of his own."

"Yeah, but that was about galvanizing people, waking them up, breaking them out of their myopia, about justice," I said. "It wasn't about the perfect Passover meal."

"You call this matzoh!" Scott replied. "And *wine*? I made better wine out of water!"

As I'm placing the last sheets on the tables, Mark trots in and asks me if I have a little time. While we talk, he tugs at a sheet, covers a hole in a queen-size with his thumb.

"Do you have enough of them?" Mark asks.

"I think so," I reply.

"You think so?" he says, incredulous. "Didn't you measure?"

I mutter something under my breath. Together, we walk into the sacristy to figure out the logistics of this evening's Eucharist. Tonight the priest blesses extra wine and bread, called the reserved sacrament, to serve tomorrow, during the Good Friday service, because the bread can't be consecrated on the day of Christ's death. We have to figure out where to put the reserved sacrament, how many wafers to bless for both services, how much wine . . . Mark pulls two pottery chalices from a cupboard in the sacristy and holds them up. "These are appropriate, don't you think?" He removes a small brass goblet with a tight, rounded lid from a little gold box behind the altar. The goblet, where the consecrated host is kept, is called a ciborium, and the box is a tabernacle, after its Jewish roots. Inside the door of the tabernacle are tiny lace curtains. I once looked over at an open tabernacle and had a sudden vision of Jesus in drag.

Mark hands me a cloth and says in his boot camp commander's voice, "Dust it out."

"I beg your pardon?" I reply.

"Dust it out, please," he snaps, and walks away.

Martha Siegel, who will preach tonight, arrives, carrying

her notes in one hand, a casserole dish in the other. Dodie Little, who heads the lay eucharistic ministers, walks in with two other LEMs. In the kitchen, Sam has covered a huge table with bowls holding puffy pancakes of bread dough in mid-rise. Lentil stew bubbles on the stove. A lump in a cheesecloth drains on a cutting board tilted into the sink. Sam has made an entire Mediterranean meal for tonight, choosing the recipes himself: lentil stew scented with rosemary, pita bread, a cheese made from milk flavored with thyme. His crowning glory is a two-and-a-half-foot challah, a braided Easter bread, baked to a dusky brown and scattered with poppy seeds. He showed it to Mark yesterday and Mark told him he would say a special prayer over it during the meal.

By five-thirty, all the servers have arrived and Dodie and I have placed two baskets of neatly folded white towels, two large stainless bowls from the kitchen, and pitchers of water next to two chairs at the far end of the room, facing the head table.

At six, a few people wander in and begin to awkwardly sit down at the tables. I rush out to the door to peer down the sidewalk. No one is there, and I become the hostess who sees a failed dinner party materializing before her eyes.

As I'm fretting at the door, two elderly women arrive.

"Look," says one of them, grabbing my arm. "Look at the light on that building." I lift my eyes and see a white building flooded with pink sunset light. She grins at me and lifts her walker over the stoop.

Suddenly the room is almost full, then near to overflowing. Mark rushes up to me.

"Let's get some card tables. Just in case," he says, and leads me down the perilous stairs into the basement. We dust off four tables and drag them up. Two of the servers hastily set them.

The light is fading outside and the candles are casting a

glow on the rows of faces at the white-covered tables. The sheets don't look too bad in this light. Mark stands up at the head table and welcomes everyone to the service. We sing, "Where charity and love prevail, there God is ever found; brought here together by Christ's love, by love are we thus bound."

After the homily, Dodie and I stand and walk over to the two chairs facing the head table. Mark invites those who want, to stand and make two lines.

Mark and Martha get up from their chairs and walk down the room toward Dodie and me. I sit down in the chair and Mark kneels in front of me. He pours water over my foot and begins a steady, vigorous scrubbing. This is not a symbolic washing. Then he takes a towel and, cradling my foot in his hands, looks up. Something cracks open and we both grin. "Thanks," he whispers, and stands up.

A dark-haired woman, Catherine, who sings in the choir, kneels before Gary, a young teacher. Catherine's daughter, Sarah, dances around them like a sprite. As Catherine pours the water over Gary's foot, she smiles up at him. They are shy, like animals.

When Catherine is finished, Gary washes her feet. Then she asks me if she may wash Sarah's feet. Sarah's tiny feet hang over the basin. She is so excited her feet are still dancing. Her mother looks up at her as she pours the water over her toes. In her eyes is an abundance and a ready sacrifice. I see that hidden in this Maundy Thursday liturgy is a message, like a note slipped into a sleeve, about how love will break our hearts.

The room is still, the air is gentle. Sometimes people embrace after they have washed each other's feet. Katrina is standing at the end of the room, barefoot. Richard Bass, a towel draped over his arm like a waiter, is helping Esther Schulz to her seat. I kneel down before a thin woman I've seen a few times at church. Her foot is nothing but stretched skin over bone. As I hold it, I realize that Jesus knew a secret: to wash someone's foot, if it is a voluntary act, engenders compassion. The lowly, unprotected foot, not the wise hands or head, is vulnerable, unmasked. I think, *There is a reason for all of this.* When everyone is finished, Mark stands up at his place and begins the Eucharist prayer. "God is within you," he says, and we reply, "And also within you."

WHEN THE EUCHARIST is finished and we have prayed, "Gracious God, thank you for feeding us in these holy mysteries . . . ," each server brings out a pot of lentils, a loaf of bread, and a round of cheese. When we have all settled down to eating, Sam sidles out of the kitchen toward my chair. "We forgot the challah," he says. "Let's just forget about it. I'm sure Mark has forgotten the prayer."

"Go get it," I say, rising.

"No, I'm sure he's forgotten," Sam repeats.

"Go get it," I reply and head up toward Mark. He puts down his fork and stands up.

Sam returns from the kitchen, bearing the challah in his arms. I push him toward Mark, between the tables. As he walks forward, someone begins to clap. And then another. Soon everyone is applauding Sam. His face is bright as he leans down and places it on the table in front of Mark, his offering, our food.

When the meal is over, we stand, gather up the flowers from the tables, and begin to sing the "Pange Lingua," a fourteenth-century plainsong to words by Thomas Aquinas: "Now my tongue the mystery telling of the glorious body sing . . ." Mark carries the reserved sacrament covered in a thin lace cloth into the church and we follow. As I walk into the church, the stone walls are particularly cold; it feels like walking into a tomb.

Mark places the sacrament inside the baptismal font, and we place the flowers on the steps all around it. Then we sing the remaining lines: "Therefore we, before him bending, this great Sacrament revere; types and shadows have their ending, for the newer rite is here; faith our outward sense befriending makes our inward vision clear."

One by one, people drop into chairs that face the font or quietly leave the church. Finally there are about ten of us left. Chris Boesch sits with her hands folded in her lap. Martha Siegel is reading John's Gospel. I close my eyes. In this dark night, Jesus went with his disciples to the garden at Gethsemane (presumably they had rented the room where they had dinner for only a few hours). He prayed, "Let this cup pass." He kept asking his disciples to stay awake and pray with him because, I realize, cutting through the veil of Bible story, Jesus was afraid. Sometime in the early hours of the morning, Roman soldiers came for him.

I sit and, in an effort to connect myself to that night, try to imagine people I love and admire being taken away in the night. Relatives of the *desaparecidos* of Argentina's Dirty War tell of coming home to a cup of tea left unfinished on the table, glasses flung on the bedroom floor. I think of the martyrs of this century: Dietrich Bonhoeffer, Nelson Mandela, Jacobo Timerman, Václav Havel.

"I believed that to be a good cleric was to be more available, more understanding," said Daniel Berrigan, the Jesuit priest and writer, in an interview with Robert Coles. "[But now] the fate of people, of the world demand[s] that one not be merely a listener, or a good friend, but yes, be in trouble."

I met Berrigan in the spring of 1986. At the time, he was appealing a three- to ten-year sentence handed down in Pennsylvania for walking into a General Electric manufacturing plant, pouring blood (his own) on a missile, and beating on the nose cone with a household hammer. In 1970–1972, he spent two years in Connecticut's Danbury Prison for destroying draft files in Catonsville, Maryland. I asked him how many times he'd been in jail and he replied, "Not enough."

Some parishes have an all-night vigil: people take turns watching and sleeping in sleeping bags on the floor. Ours will end at midnight. I drift into sleep and wake when someone laughs aloud on the porch outside.

ON GOOD FRIDAY at noon, I meet George Barrett and Ann Jaqua on the sidewalk outside the church. We say very little to each other, then walk in together. The crucifix is draped in black. Below the crucifix, the tabernacle door is flung open, revealing an empty box. A few people are scattered in the pews. In a few minutes, Mark Asman and Anne Howard, dressed in black cassocks, walk through the sacristy door into the sanctuary and sit down.

For the next three hours, they take turns reading from Leonardo Boff, a Latin American Roman Catholic priest, who has written a meditation for each of the fourteen Stations of the Cross. Boff is a Brazilian liberation theologian. His Stations are written to remind his listeners that sin cannot be relegated only to the personal and private. The Church has put too much emphasis on personal sins, Boff would say, and ignored the greater sin of collaboration with the powerful. The poor don't get that way by accident.

"Where do we find God?" Boff asks. "In prayer, in the interior life, unselfishness, in the Sacraments, in loving connection with our neighbors? What we learn from Jesus is different. We learn, Where does God want to be encountered by human beings? In the faces of the humiliated."

As I sit in the pew, I remember a man in Nicaragua walking beside the road, carrying a bundle of logs. He was bent over so completely his hands brushed his bare ankles.

I intend to stay at the service only an hour, but the readings, the prayers between them, and the silence slowly pull me in. I feel as if I'm a stone dropping through water toward the floor of a lake.

"The Tenth Station: Jesus is stripped of his garments."

"His clothes were not given to his relatives. His tunic was raffled off in a dice game," reads Mark. "He died in this way so that those who came after him would never feel alone in their suffering."

"The Eleventh Station: Jesus is nailed to the cross."

"Jesus was crucified, not because of a whim, but because of the way the world is organized," reads Anne. "It rejected Jesus and eliminated him. But it is God's will to establish the Kingdom in the midst of creation. God does not cease to will it."

"The Fourteenth Station: Jesus is placed in the tomb."

". . . life blossoms into full flower only in those who nurture life here on this earth," Mark reads. "In those who defend its rights, protect its dignity, and are even willing to accept death in their witness to it. . . . All those who died like Jesus, sacrificing their lives out of love . . . will inherit life in all its fullness. . . . It is thanks to them that history goes on as a pageant of hope."

At the end, we sing, "Were you there when they crucified my Lord? Were you there when they laid him in the tomb?" Anne and Mark leave the sanctuary. What is left is the empty tabernacle and its open door.

IN THE LAST fifteen years, a renewal of interest in the "historical Jesus" has resulted in books, papers, and arguments as to who this person really was. The Jesus in the Gospels is a figure compiled by men who lived long after him and who looked back through the muddy lens of the early church, with all its needs, rivalries, and axes to grind. Yet scholars now believe that it's possible to at least come close to Jesus' reality, to some of his real words and actions, through painstaking examination of the Gospels and comparisons between them and other recently discovered documents, like the Nag Hammadi texts, fourth-century manuscripts buried in pottery jars near the Nile River and dug up in 1945. The Jesus Seminar is a group of religious scholars who actually vote on what words and events in the Gospels can be ascribed to Jesus. Many of its members have written books, including John Dominic Crossan, a professor of biblical studies at DePaul University in Chicago, and Marcus Borg, a professor of religious studies at Oregon State University.

Both Borg and Crossan think that as Jesus traveled from town to town, healing and preaching, he lived an itinerant's life. He seems to have deliberately placed himself just outside the reach of the Roman empire. The way he lived spoke. As Harvey Guthrie, the former dean of the Episcopal Divinity School in Cambridge, put it, "Jesus' life said: You can live like this and it's okay. In fact, this is the kingdom of God."

His life was marked by an activity radical for his day, or for ours: Jesus sat down with what Crossan calls "nuisances and nobodies." To know with whom people eat, Crossan points out, is to be shown a map to social hierarchy. Jesus made no distinctions or discriminations; his was the open table. Crossan calls it "an open commensality."

The poor and the oppressed live with two dreams, says Crossan: "One is quick revenge—a world in which they might get in turn to put their boots on those other necks. Another is reciprocal justice—a world in which there would never again be any boots on any necks."

The religious leaders of first-century Jerusalem lived by a purity code that not only classified food and habits but classified people into rigid categories: sinners, untouchables, outcasts . . . People who were sick or maimed were not "whole," and therefore not "pure." It was a world, as Borg describes it, "with sharp social boundaries between pure and impure, righteous and sinner, whole and not whole, male and female, rich and poor, Jew and Gentile." Jesus refused to live by it.

For the first five months of the Kitchen's life, we handed the soup through a little window cut into the back door of the parish hall. The men and women stood in line outside. Then the winter came, and the rains. Volunteers from the Presbyterian Church were the first to protest. Why can't the people come inside? they said. It's cold, it's wet; we feel uncomfortable; we're dry and warm and they are miserable and cold. Finally, we let them in once, for a sit-down meal with the brothers from Mount Calvary. Everyone behaved, no fights broke out. In fact, they were too well behaved. Almost no one spoke. Tables of silent men filled the hall. They ate and left. After that, it seemed silly not to just let them in. For months, they sat at the tables and ate and we stood behind the serving table, or bustled between them, carrying trays. We ate before we arrived, or standing up in the kitchen. Then one day, I noticed that at a table with four men in various states of homelessness was a well-dressed woman, eating the same food. She was, I realized, a volunteer from the Latter-Day Saints. The next week, I tried it. I sat down, awkwardly, at a table with six men. A few of them nodded. Others stared ahead. The World Series was on, and the previous night's game had been a particularly exciting one: the longest in Series history. I was happy to have a conversation opener I was sure we all shared.

"See the game last night?" I said, expectantly.

Several pairs of eyes turned toward me. No one spoke. Finally, a huge man with an Abe Lincoln beard, whom I later came to know as Alan, asked, "What game?"

"The World Series," I replied.

"Oh, is that on now?" he said.

"Yeah," I said, less confident now. "It was a great game."

"I don't actually watch TV," said another of the men. "I prefer reading."

"Yeah," Alan agreed. "Or I watch PBS. There's a good series on German Expressionism on right now."

One day, I arrived to work in the soup kitchen hungry, dirty, and dressed in old sweats. I joined the line of men without checking in with the Kitchen manager, and as I received my soup, I looked straight into the volunteer's eyes. They shone with pity. I began to explain, then thought better of it. I sat down at a table with Greg and Alan. Greg said, "What did Robin Hood say to Maid Marian when she asked him if he wanted to live with her in the forest?"

"I don't know," I replied.

"Sure would," he said, and I laughed.

COMMENSALITY, IN COMPARISON with the purity code, was so minimal a practice as to be almost nonexistent. One was elaborate, divisive, and hierarchical, a construction; the other was simple, a kind of nothing, a deconstruction. People who had a lot of power couldn't see it. Jesus would say, The Sabbath is made for people, not people for the Sabbath, and a Pharisee would reply, Yes, but why don't your disciples wash between courses? The people who saw it right away were those with nothing, those who didn't exist: the outcast woman who anointed Jesus' feet with her hair at a dinner party; Bartimaeus, the blind beggar. The possibly psychotic Magdalene.

After I'd eaten at the tables with the men and women for a couple of months, when I walked in the door, I began to feel as if I were walking through a curtain. I felt light-headed; I had the bends. One day, as I handed a guy a bowl of soup, an image of a river of vegetables flowing into and then out of the soup kitchen filled me up. My role was to catch the vegetables, make them into soup, and then pass them along. I thought about how weird it would be to charge for the soup: what was freely given had to be freely given away. A phrase came to my mind, in the way notices used to come over teletype machines, word by word: "the economy of abundance."

As the Kitchen grew and developed, I discovered the economy of abundance to be a world both tenuous and surprising. Because we couldn't buy our way out, we had to rely on what was given, whatever it was. Unexpected gifts, like cubes of frozen cheddar, a box of frozen bologna, a gallon of sour cream salad dressing, were causes for celebration.

We scrounged for a living. We begged bread from local bakeries; from butchers, we begged the chicken breast bones left after most of the breast is removed; from traveling executives, we accepted the soaps and shampoos collected in hotels. On the bottom rungs, scrounging is a craft, a way of life. The men we served in the Kitchen sifted through wastebaskets at the end of the day, finding a box of gold hairpins, a half-smoked cigarette, two paper clips. Everything is useful, nothing is wasted. I came to believe that "scrounge" is one of God's verbs. A pregnant, unmarried woman; tax collectors, blind beggars, a son conceived out of wedlock. God uses what is useless, what is discarded, "things low and contemptible, mere nothings, to overthrow the existing order." At the end of my shift one day Larry asked me what I was planning to do with a box of nearly black bananas.

"I'm going to throw them away."

"Oh, no," he replied, "you can't do that."

"Why not?"

"Because those are righteous bananas, Nora," he said. "I'm going to make banana cream pies."

One morning I ran out of fruit in the Kitchen at just the moment a farmer drove up with three cases of oranges.

It happened over and over again: I had no volunteers on a

President's Day holiday, and Isabelle Walker-Klein called the church to ask if we needed any help. The steering committee of the Kitchen was sitting around in the church library lamenting our lack of funds one December, and Ann Jaqua went to her box and found a check from a local foundation for $2,500.

After his conversion, St. Francis saw "everything upside down," said Frank Rogers, Jr., a theologian at the School of Theology at Claremont. "He was not enamored of the strength and security of well-guarded towers, walled city states and impressive cathedrals. Rather he saw everything hanging over nothing. And he was astonished, but grateful, that everything did not fall down."

I didn't understand how these things happened at the Kitchen, but I began to rely on them. We stopped worrying too much about fund-raising, kept our expenses low, and waited to see what would happen next. In this atmosphere a wild freedom flourished; we could run on nothing. The Kitchen had what a friend, Christina Fernandez, called a "radical serenity."

Not that it lasted in me. I would make soup for a hundred and fifty out of discarded carrots and then go home and worry about my 401K. I would sit down at the table with Alan, Greg, and the boys and I would feel free, as if all of me were there, including the parts I normally hide in company, and the parts so marginalized inside myself that I didn't even know who or what they were, and then I would drive around in my new red Volvo 850 and feel contemptuous toward someone driving a Honda. At those times, as Anne Lamott writes, "I know Jesus drinks himself to sleep."

Still, when I recited the Nicene Creed on Sunday morning, the "unseen" became for me, not a realm of ghosts, but an ignored otherness, a place where you waited and hoped. It was fragile and at the same time luminous. It was as if we were sneaking in under the radar.

ON GOOD FRIDAY EVENING, I return to church. Holy
Week's liturgies, one after the other, have begun to accumulate
in me. Each service of the Triduum strips away a layer of
defensive, outer cells. The whole church is organized in a cycle
of seasons, liturgies, holy days, and Gospel readings that may
be connected to how life unfolds. We need to revisit our experience over and over again; each time, each visit, another layer
is peeled away, another piece or aspect is revealed. Our cells
carry memories that rise on anniversaries, demand another
look. Holy Week is a distillation of this repetition. Each Good
Friday, every year, we look again. The result is a reordering of
experience. Ann Jaqua said once at the base community that
after she'd walked in the wilderness for several weeks, after her
body finally got used to the forty-pound pack and the high
mountain passes, her thoughts settled, "like sand in a cen-
trifuge, each layer taking its rightful place. What I had thought
was important was not important. What had seemed to be of
minor significance was now on top."

In the Good Friday evening service everything is stripped
away; only the cross remains, the barest wood. Tonight's service has at its center the veneration of that cross. We will be
invited to go forward and touch or kiss its wood or the figure
hanging there.

Getting down to the cross. Each service has led us here;
each one has stripped away the layers until we arrive at Good
Friday, bare and exposed, staking our lives on this peculiar
wrenching death. St. John of the Cross said it is sometimes
easier to see in the darkness than in the light.

The choir enters in silence and disperses throughout the
congregation; two priests in cassocks, Mark Asman and Ev
Simson, walk to the altar area and sit down. Ev, a retired priest

who now visits prisoners at the federal maximum-security prison in Lompoc, will preach.

Tonight the Gospel is John's version of the Passion of Jesus, from the arrival of the Roman soldiers at the garden, to the death of Jesus on the cross. The choir sings the whole Passion. Lisa Rutherford, who has a beautiful soprano voice, sings the part of Jesus. When the time arrives for the narrator to describe what happened after Jesus died, Grey Brothers breaks into a plaintive Gregorian chant that fills the church with fragile, high notes.

In his sermon, Ev says there were no crucifixions in Rome itself, only in the provinces; it was a punishment reserved for rural troublemakers, thieves, those who were not considered "people." The Nazis called Jews "Figuren," "Stücke," "dolls," "wood," "merchandise," "rags."

The intent of crucifixion was to do more than kill. It was to dismantle the human person. "Torture" derives from the Latin word meaning "to twist."

Sitting in the pew, I shiver like a child.

When Ev preaches, he grips the pulpit with his left hand and sways. He was once dean of the Episcopal cathedral in Los Angeles. The pressure of the job built up so much in him that he had to resign. He promised himself he would not do that to himself again and so, as he interviewed in parishes for another job, he told them the truth: "I am a priest in need of healing," he said. One by one, parishes passed him up, until he came to the one in Monrovia, a suburb of L.A. "I am a priest in need of healing," he said to the search committee.

"And we are a church in need of healing," they replied, and hired him.

"We take our cross to his cross," Ev preaches. "The cross I wear around my neck is from the Order of the Holy Cross. 'Holy' means complete. A holy cross makes us whole. Amen."

He turns from the pulpit and sits down. After the prayers, he and Mark walk to the crucifix above the altar and remove it from the wall. They carry it through the sacristy door and out of the church. They come back in through the front entrance; Ev carries the crucifix up the aisle. Mark follows him. Three times they stop. Mark chants:

"Behold the wood of the cross on which was hung the world's salvation." Behold everything hanging over nothing.

When they arrive at the steps leading to the altar, two acolytes take the cross and hold it upright. Ev kneels in front of the cross, leans forward, and kisses the feet of Jesus. Mark follows him. I watch as men and women slowly leave their pews. They are like figures in a modern Passion play. A young woman, in a close-fitted velvet cap, her hair gone because of chemotherapy, her face puffy from steroid injections, all of this to hunt and kill her brain tumor.

A professor at the local city college, tall and redheaded, whose mother has lived with her for the last eight years and now may have to be placed in a nursing home.

Lois Hitz, beautiful, her dark hair brushing her cheek bones.

An older woman who is considering coming out of the closet. A woman who struggles with depression. An autistic man. Shadows in the dark.

I think as I watch them standing in line that I have known this community for six years, sensed its rhythms, watched it sow and harvest. I am all bound up in them.

I kneel down in front of the cross. I've come full circle from Ash Wednesday, on my knees for the imposition of ashes, to kneeling here to kiss the cross. I am marked here, in the same way I was marked with ashes, in the same way I was marked at my baptism. As my lips meet the wood, I'm pierced by a shaft of pain so tender I sob. A last layer cracks.

I see the faces of the men in the soup kitchen, those human

beings made into rags, into debris. Their faces shine here at the cross in a way that no other faces do. They know what this man hanging here has suffered, as he knows their suffering. He was made into trash here on the cross; his body was probably eaten by dogs.

The parts of myself that are alive among those men are the parts I hide everywhere else. Crazy, inarticulate, imperfect, in need. The person humiliated by simply being born a woman. How often I apologize, desire to please. All the parts of myself that I colonize, make into trash. In the darkness, I see them, hidden in my shadows, and I understand then how it is that seeing them makes me whole.

ON HOLY SATURDAY MORNING Vincent and I rise early and go off to the local farmers' market. There, amid masses of people buying early spring peas, baby lettuces, and bouquets of Easter lilies, I move slowly and can't remember the right words for things. I've been traveling for two days now in the mysteries and I'm disoriented, jet-lagged.

On this day, between Good Friday and Easter, nothing happens. Jesus is dead. All movement stops. It is hard to endure, but I am reminded of a talk given by David Richo, a former Jesuit priest and a therapist, about our fragmented lives, our grief and depression and the need to simply be held in that state.

"It is like the Pietà, Mary holding the broken body of Jesus," Richo said. "Just her holding it [the body] that way, that moment of pause at the foot of the cross, when she holds him in his broken, fragmented state, and loves him even this way . . . that's how she prepared him for his resurrection."

In the afternoon, I drop by Trinity for an hour to watch them decorate for this evening and for Easter Sunday. Several Flower Guild women have ringed the paschal candle stand with flowers. Ann Jaqua and I are admiring it when Mark arrives, his black suit smudged with dust, a cloth in one hand.

"Ah," he says, gripping the stand. "I think I'll wash it."

"Oh, be careful," Ann says. "Those flowers are fragile."

"It'll be all right," he says in male-ese. He picks up the stand and all the flowers fall off.

A beat of silence.

"Here," Ann says finally, "let me fix it."

"Nope," says Mark. "I did it. I'll fix it. Just give me some pointers."

"Put the greens on first," Ann says smiling, and walks away.

Later Vincent and I visit friends at a house up the coast. I sit outside on a deck overlooking the ocean, sleepy and not quite there, talking to a friend about the soup kitchen. Another guest, a woman whose hair is only inches long, enters the conversation.

"What is it you do?" she asks.

I tell her something about the Kitchen.

"And why do you work there?"

"Because of my faith," I reply, hoping she won't run away.

"What is your faith?" she asks. I try to tell her, without using words that might or might not have meaning or, worse, be overloaded with the wrong meaning.

"I have a lot of questions," I finally mumble.

"What have you resolved?" she asks.

"Uh," I reply. "Not much."

"Well, what have you resolved?" she asks again. I'm too embarrassed to really get into it. I mutter something vague and she looks away. In a little while, she gets up to leave. She lurches as she rises. She's been gone about twenty minutes when I register her question—"Well, what have you resolved?"—and put it together with the nearly bald head, a head just like my brother's.

WHEN I ARRIVE at church Saturday night, I feel drunk on liturgy, as if I will awake sprawled in some sacristy somewhere, hung over.

The Easter Vigil begins in the dark. From the back of the church, Mark Asman lights a dish of charcoal with a flint. From the fire a deacon lights the paschal candle. She sings, "The light of Christ."

The deacon leads the procession up the aisle, holding the candle. From it we all light little candles. The church is beautiful in this simple light.

Every life must be retold and remade. The Easter Vigil retells the history of Christianity, from Genesis—"In the beginning when God created the heavens and the earth, the earth was a formless void"—to the Exodus, to the moment when Magdalene, gone to the tomb, is greeted by an angel who says, "I know you are looking for Jesus who was crucified. He is not here."

It is a history of this other world, this "different order." In the darkness, lit only by our own frail candles, we sit and listen to how the Spirit "brooded" over the face of the waters; how the dove returned to Noah with an olive leaf in its beak; how Abraham lifted his knife over his son; how Moses stretched his staff over the sea.

In almost every language except English the same word is used for the Jewish Passover and the Christian Easter: pascha, passover. This is the night that Jesus passes over from death into life; this is the night when people are traditionally baptized, drowned to the old life, to insensibility and unconsciousness, and risen into a new life, into compassion, availability, abundance.

Tonight Robin, from our base community, will enter the

waters to drown. The whole base community are her god-parents; we sit behind Robin and her family.

When we are finished with the long Hebrew Scripture lessons, Mark invites us all to renew our baptismal vows by answering together a series of questions: "Do you reaffirm your renunciation of evil and renew your commitment to Jesus Christ?

"Will you seek and serve Christ in all persons, loving your neighbor as yourself?

"Will you strive for justice and peace among all people, and respect the dignity of every human being?"

Then Robin and the others who will be baptized rise and march down the aisle toward the baptismal font with Mark. She looks expectant, brave.

"I baptize you in the name of the Father," says Mark, pouring water over her dark hair. "And of the Son," another splash. "And of the Holy Spirit. Amen." Damp, she smiles up at him. He gives her a hug. An acolyte takes the silver bowl of water out of the font and hands it to Robin, who then walks up the aisle. In front of the altar, Robin turns, holding out the bowl of water like an offering.

One by one, we go up to Robin and "renew our vows" by crossing ourselves with the water. As I dip my hand into the bowl, I look into Robin's face and remember the first time she came to the base community, a little knot of a girl. The young woman who meets my eyes is serene, enrolled in a master's program in education at the university, student-teaching in a high school.

In his sermon, George Barrett says, "Tonight, we look over our shoulders at our history. We look over our shoulders at Jesus and at where we have been.

"Now your history is bound to the history of God. And you are marked as Christ's own forever." Then George looks straight at Robin and the others. "Will you strive for justice and peace?" he asks. "Will you respect the dignity of every human being?"

"When I first came here, my life was like plowing a hard field," Robin said to the base community. "Everything was broken up. Then, it lay fallow. Now, I am growing."

"Our Robin," says Mark Benson tonight. "Our Robin."

Eastertide

ANN JAQUA WAS sitting on a Trailways bus heading into Washington D.C., when she looked up from the book she was reading and believed in the resurrection. "I was saying the Creed from the daily office with the prayer book open on my lap and looking out the window at the telephone poles and trees zipping by. When I came to the words, 'I believe in the resurrection,' I don't know what happened, but my guard went down, I guess. I really believed it completely for an instant. I mean I knew without a doubt that it was true. I was in a pretty black depression over the lives of my daughters. I thought they were all headed for disaster. In that instant what I knew was that all my rational ideas about my children, all the things I'd learned from my parents and the Church about 'If you do that, this will follow,' were not necessarily true. The rules didn't hold. It was just enough to allow me to let go of my terrible fear, to see the goodness in my children and to believe in their potential for good. The resurrection means that nothing is hopeless anymore."

ON EASTER SUNDAY, I end up on the stone steps of the baptismal font in the back of the church, the only seat left in the house. Surrounding me are uncertain, dressed–up strangers who look like bewildered tourists in a new city, consulting the bulletin as if it were a map. Many of them are clutching the hand of a child.

The procession begins with an acolyte holding high the paschal candle, followed by another acolyte swinging the incense-filled thurible. He makes it halfway down the aisle before several people begin to sneeze and cough. The choir sings, "Jesus Christ is risen today, alleluia!" A little girl cries to her mother, "The music is too loud!" Her mother says to a friend, "They don't have much in the way of kneeling." The priests flow by, in white robes embroidered in lush, shiny gold. Soon they are all massed at the altar with hundreds of Easter lilies, banks of gold and white.

The beautiful robes, the flowers, and the music disguise— the way the sweet scent of lilies masks the smell of the dead—the bizarre story we are about to hear. During what is called the sequence hymn, a covey of acolytes carry the paschal candle, two candlesticks, and the Gospel from the altar area down the main aisle into the center of the church. Mark follows. A third of the way down they stop. Mark takes the Gospel from the acolyte, lifts it above the child's head, and says, "The Holy Gospel of our Lord Jesus Christ according to Luke.

"On the first day of the week, at early dawn," he reads, "the women came to the tomb, taking the spices that they had prepared. They found the stone rolled away from the tomb, but when they went in, they did not find the body. While they were perplexed about this, suddenly two men in dazzling clothes stood beside them. The women were terrified and bowed their faces to the ground, but the men said to them, 'Why do you look for the living among the dead?' "

As Mark reads, I contemplate those women: Mary Magdalene, Joanna, and the woman known only as Mary, the mother of James. They came to the tomb to embalm a body, a woman's job in first-century Jerusalem. I imagine them getting ready to walk out to the caves, numb with grief, preparing themselves for a painful but familiar job.

I watch the light falling on the acolyte's fair hair. Very suddenly, so suddenly I take a sharp breath, the story moves into me. This morning, before I came to church, and the reason I was so late, I had a fight with Vincent. It was one of those stupid marital fights in which things escalate so fast you're left with your head spinning, and words come out of your mouth you cannot believe. Worse, I provoked it. Worse yet, I provoked it because I was lonely. This is my story; I work against myself. I enact and reenact old, painful patterns. Preserve the past, embalm the dead. In the early days of therapy, I thought, Well, now I know about this, I'll change. To my astonishment, it was nearly impossible. I had formed a complete self around unconscious, simple rules: I won't get what I need; I have to solve everyone's problems; it's better to build up resentment, provoke a fight, and then lick my wounds in private.

In the work of therapy, as the old rules and their origins surfaced like dark, drowned ships, I began to see possibility. In his essay "A Note on Story," James Hillman, a Jungian analyst, writes about how the patient and analyst work together to "rewrite the case history into a new story." Hillman continues, "Some of the healing that goes on, maybe even the essence of it is this collaborative 'fiction,' this putting all the chaotic and traumatic events of a life into a new story."

While the rewriting went on in the therapist's office, sometimes my behavior changed and sometimes it didn't. When things went well—when I said to Vincent, "I miss you," rather than "Why are you so distant?"—it was as if I had found an antidote to poison. These experiences built up in me, into memory, making a place and a voice inside myself that was less anxious, more forgiving, and had a longer sense of time. But it was slow work, painstakingly slow, and each new act, especially in the beginning, involved a risk. That tomb is empty without the past to fill it. My new behavior got good results, but it necessitated a new identity. I didn't always know who I was, even or especially when things felt good. If the old rules didn't hold, how was I to understand my life? If the vantage point from which I looked back at my history changed, then the history itself was new. Often it was easier, less frightening, just to slip back into the painful but familiar past. "Her cookin's lousy and her hands are clammy," Tom Lehrer's song goes, "But what the hell, it's home."

If I had been with those women, I think today, I would have wanted to drop my spices and run. Not because I was afraid of those dazzling suits, but because I was afraid of that new life.

"He is not here," Mark reads, "but has risen."

BELIEF AND DISBELIEF in the resurrection trade places in my heart like "watchmen taking shifts," as the writer Paul Elie puts it. I've known for years that even those words—"belief" and "disbelief"—don't really describe what I think when I think about the resurrection. Something happened to him, is the way I put it to myself. Something happens to me.

In the mid-eighties, I visited a dinosaur dig with Vincent's aunt, Malinda Chouinard, her children, and a friend. The dig was in eastern Montana, on the edge of the prairie that had once been an inland sea. We slept in huge white tepees, getting up in the night to watch the Northern Lights sprinkle the sky with pink powder. During the day we fished for pieces of dinosaur egg in the clay soil with toothbrushes and dentists' fine-pointed tools. The largest egg fragment I found was a quarter-inch wide, coal black and finely pitted like the rind of an orange. It was a hundred million years old. All around us were pieces of egg and bone—fragments, nothing made sense.

Each evening, a paleontologist described what they had made of these bits and pieces, how they saw mother dinosaurs on nests, dinosaurs that lived in herds, their duckbills, their webbed feet. Listening to him was like watching a weaver make whole cloth out of threads or a pot emerge from shards.

When I ponder the resurrected Jesus, what I see is this coherence, this possibility. Out of the chaos and trauma of death, something new is written or revealed. Jesus walked through the curtain, into the Reality blazing behind it, a place he had grasped and apprehended all his life. Then, because he lived fully in hope, fully in love, something happened to him. Nothing kept him, nothing held onto him, the past didn't weigh him down. He returned, more coherent, more real, carrying Reality with him, in a final act of love. Jesus, as archaeologist, picked up the pieces, made them cohere, gave them meaning, and knitted, finally, everything together. Nothing is hopeless anymore.

Then the watchmen take their shifts. On those Montana nights, as I listened with friends and family to the paleontologists' talks, I would think, This is amazing, and then, How do we know if it's true? So much theory from so little evidence. I contemplate the resurrection and think, We could be making all of this up, sitting here in the pews. The Mass as mass psychosis.

The people in front of me stand up one by one and walk forward to the communion rail. I get up to join them. Whether or not I believe in the resurrection makes no difference if I don't make a different life. We are the ongoing story. The priest in Ignazio Silone's *Bread and Wine* says, "If we live like him, it will be as if he never died."

IN THE BASE COMMUNITY we fish in the shards of the Eastertide Gospels. The post-Easter stories describe events at once outrageous and completely ordinary. At the end of John's Gospel, Simon Peter and some of the disciples are back at work. They've been up all night on a boat out on the sea but haven't caught anything. In the early hours of the morning, a man on the beach calls out to them to throw their nets on the right side of the boat. So many fish are caught they can barely haul them in. One of the disciples points to the man and says, "It is the Lord." Peter leaps into the water and swims to shore. There Jesus has got a fire going. He says to Peter, "Bring some of those fish over here. Come and have breakfast."

In Luke, after appearing suddenly among the terrified disciples, Jesus says, "Does anyone have anything to eat?"

While two men walk toward Emmaus, a village seven miles from Jerusalem, another man joins them. "Their hearts burn within them," but it isn't until they are eating together that evening, until he breaks bread, "that their eyes were opened."

Thomas the Twin must put his fingers not on, but inside Jesus' rib cage before he apprehends, before he gets it.

None of the Eastertide images are airy or abstract. They are about eating, walking, touch. Implicit in them is the intimacy of bodily life, its need for food and touch, and its terrible vulnerability to suffering. The Christ comes to us in the flesh, in our beloved skin and bone.

"What if someone we loved came back from the dead?" Mark Benson asks on the Thursday of Easter week.

"If it were Mark Asman he would say, 'You snooze, you lose,' " says Dodie.

"If one of us died and came back alive, and we heard about it," Ann Jaqua says, "what would we do? We might believe that the person were God and we might want to pray to that person as we once had to God."

"It would make me nervous," Elizabeth says.

Later, as we say compline, I let my attention fall on each of them—Ann, Elizabeth, Dodie, Mark—and find that my love for them is felt as a clear seeing of them and as a sense of having been seen by them and been warmed by the sight, touched.

Afterward, I walk Lois to her car, a white four-wheel-drive Suzuki. She and Ben drive on rough roads deep into the desert. I ask her how's she doing.

"Not very well," she replies.

"This must be a drag, Lois," I blurt out, and then think, That was inane.

"It's a drag, Nora," she says fiercely. "It's a real drag."

THE FOLLOWING MONDAY, a week after Easter, I'm working in my studio when Vincent interrupts, a sorrowful look on his face. My hand goes to my throat.

"No," he says. "Ephraim."

Chris Boesch has called to tell us that Ephraim was found downtown last night, lying comatose in a gutter, and taken to Cottage Hospital, where he died several hours later of "drug toxicity." His family was with him: his sister, Ida, and his stepmother and father from Bakersfield. I call Chris back. She says, "I remember what he taught me, some of which I didn't want to know."

On Tuesday morning in the soup kitchen, we do an impromptu memorial for him. Mikel Morrison, a deacon who was an early program director of the Kitchen, talks about his life with us and says a few prayers. Very few of the men who knew him are there, but a new man in town, Tim, thanks Mikel for "remembering someone who died on the streets."

Nancee Cline writes a eulogy in the church newsletter: "Ephraim used to sing to me. In the middle of making my ten-gallon wilted fruit salads, he would appear at my side, glowing with some inner joy, sing some sweet emotional song with tears in his eyes, then fade back into the bustle of the last minute preparations."

After Ephraim's service, I drop into the church office to check my vestry mailbox and see the secretary, Rachel, working through the open door. I wave at her and am about to leave, when she calls me over.

"Have you heard about the Brothers baby?" she asks.

"No," I say.

"Something is wrong," Rachel says and fills me in.

On Easter Sunday, Carrie spoke to Lori Harris, who lost a child late in pregnancy, because this baby, due in a month, was not as active as her other two had been at this late date. Lori told Carrie to go to the doctor. Carrie's doctors immediately did a sonogram and found that the baby's heart was enlarged. They also took amniotic fluid and discovered that some of her chromosomes weren't "right." Carrie and Grey were given two options: have a C-section now or wait until the due date. The baby might not survive labor. Carrie and Grey met with Martha Siegel, who has taught classes on biomedical ethics and is a nurse as well as a priest. Among many things, Martha told them to talk to the baby. They told Martha her name was Merith. Finally, Carrie and Grey decided they wanted a further test on Merith's chromosomes.

On Thursday morning, Mark Asman and I are working in the library at Trinity when the phone rings. We look at each other. Mark says, "I don't want to answer that phone," and gets up to answer it. Carrie, having sensed no activity on the part of the child, went to the hospital this morning, where they found that Merith had died. Carrie is calling from Westmont College where she went with her two little girls to find Grey. Mark clamps the phone against his shoulder, takes his calendar out of his pocket, and grabs a prayer book.

Thursday evening, as we settle in for the base community, Grey arrives to rehearse the choir. His face is creased with sorrow. The choir gathers around him, making soft clucking sounds, while he weeps.

On Friday, Carrie has to have labor induced. She and Grey hold Merith before giving her up to be cremated. On Saturday, they go up to La Cumbre Peak behind Santa Barbara with the girls and scatter Merith's ashes. They release a green balloon.

On Sunday the whole parish is mournful. Mark dedicates the Eucharist to Ephraim and Merith. Martha Siegel cries while she serves communion. Betty Bickel keeps a list of everyone who is making meals for the Brothers family and finally has to turn people away.

Nancee writes, "Merith was dearly wanted; she was infinitely precious to her parents."

EARLY IN MAY, Vincent and I fly to New York for a week to visit friends who live in a loft in Hell's Kitchen. Just before I leave, the monks at Mount Calvary ask if I have a church to go to while in the city. I shake my head and think, This is their job—to make sure I know where the gas stations are. Nick rushes down to his room to find the name of a church he visited when he was last there. "St. John's in the Village," he yells from the bottom of the stairs.

The city is damp and beautiful. The neighborhood our friends live in is clean of crack for the first time in years. We wake in the morning to a landscape of city buildings on one side, the Hudson on the other. One day, Vincent and I walk from the apartment to the Village, passing The General Theological Seminary on the way, Mark Asman's alma mater. In its courtyard, ringed by redbrick buildings, pink and white peonies are blooming. The chapel is subdued, the pews, cross, and pulpit made of dark, heavy wood. When Mark was a student here only men were ordained. Now on the faculty lists, I read "The Reverend Joanne McWilliam."

In Chelsea, we pass a group of kids on the street, mixed race, eleven or twelve years old. "When Myra lies, her nose grows," says one, exuberantly. Myra, a tall girl with braids on top of her head, looks hurt. The others realize it; a sort of shiver runs through them. A boy finally says to a girl, "Wendy, defend her!" Wendy replies, "That is not my job." I'm admiring the girl, when the boy says, "You're her friend, goddammit."

On Sunday I go to Mass at St. John's in the Village, a square brick building with floor-to-ceiling translucent windows on the street. The small altar area is knee-deep in clergy: a tense young woman subdeacon, a frosty woman deacon, and a male priest with a jocular manner. The parishioners sit subdued in cathedral chairs—interlocking padded chairs that are comfortable and movable, but make me feel too isolated and individual for the communal setting. The only lay participation in the service happens when the Prayers of the People are sung by the choirmaster.

Early in the week, Vincent and I walk from the base of Wall Street uptown. We stop in at every church we pass, from Trinity Wall Street, one of the oldest Episcopal churches in the country, to St. Patrick's Roman Catholic Cathedral, to St. Thomas's Episcopal on Fifth Avenue.

Each of the Episcopal churches is elegant, austere, and empty. At St. Patrick's, however, we see immediately the ancient culture of the Roman Catholic Church and its wide embrace: people of all ages and descriptions walk around, kneel to pray, light candles, and stand talking under the plaster statues.

Before I leave—Vincent will stay a week longer to see friends in New England—we visit a show of illuminated manuscripts at the Morgan Library. The manuscripts—Gospels and Books of Hours—are from Armenia, France, Italy, Iran, illuminated by priests and scribes in tempera, gold leaf, and what looks like simple watercolor. My favorite is one from Tours, a Book of Hours in Latin with a narrow drawing of a beautiful green-and-white shallot along its left-hand edge. On the plant is a small blue fly. It's as if a master scribe was overcome with delight at something small that played against the larger mystery of the words he was copying—the "Gloria patri et filio"—and couldn't resist pairing them for eternity. I buy a postcard of it for Lois Hitz.

When I return from New York, I call her right away. Ben answers the phone. He says Lois's tumor has cut off the entry to her stomach; she can't eat. Her pain and discomfort were so great last week that he took her to the hospital. Now she's home. Her options are two: surgery to bypass the tumor, or "nothing." Surgery might gain her six months. If "nothing," he says, then "No food, just morphine . . ." The surgery may not be successful: they may open her up and discover nothing can be done. This could leave her worse off than she is now. Lois has asked her family to come up and talk—tonight. He says he thinks—and here he begins to cry—that she has already made up her mind. He says he wants her to do the surgery, but he is not her. He says she is doing everything with great style. Her "indomitable will."

At the base community that night we take the postcard drawing of the shallot, and during compline each person holds it in his or her hands. A stillness falls on the room, like a light spring rain.

Dodie says, "I can see that days were not just days to her, they were Time."

In the morning I drive downtown to Lois and Ben's walled adobe house. Ben calls to me to come in, and I walk through the spotless blue-tiled kitchen to their bedroom. Lois and Ben's daughter, Dee, and son, Sam, are standing beside the bed look-ing shell-shocked. Lois is lying in bed, looking pretty well, hooked up to an IV and a bag of nutrients. I sit down on the bed; it's iron with a greenish hue. French doors look out to the garden. Ben is putting away towels and sheets.

"Do you put these away in the drawers or fold them on the

shelves?" he calls to her. He comes into the room, carrying a sweatshirt. "Do you put these on the shelves in the closet?" He stands uncomfortably by the bed, looking down at me. I am, incongruously, holding on to Lois's foot under the covers.

One by one the children and Ben leave the room and I have a few minutes with Lois.

"I'm not sure what to do," she says.

"This is the hardest decision you've ever made."

"It is. It is."

"But you have made hard decisions all your life. It is not as if you didn't have practice."

She nods. "But none of them have been like this. Most of the family want me to have the surgery, and I suppose I will if I am up to it. I'm concerned, though, about the treatment afterward; the doctor has no plan for treatment afterward." She hesitates, then adds, "They say it will give me six months. The last six months were pretty good. I'd take another six. I saw my grandchild walk. My daughter said, 'Don't you want to see him talk?' "

I offer to pray with her. God help Lois make this decision, I think, as we pray. I don't understand until much later, as I'm driving away, that she needed me to go out on a limb with her and be responsible, with her, for making what may have been the wrong decision. She needed me to help carry the load. I didn't. That had nothing to do with respecting Lois's autonomy; it was about washing my hands. We pretend to respect the autonomy of people who are sick or dying; in actuality, we hang them out to dry. I see something then, just at the periphery, about faith. I want to remain clean, innocent, above the fray, but faith requires me to get down and dirty, to risk making a mistake for the sake of another, to join in the awful intimacy of Lois's suffering.

. . .

ON WEDNESDAY, the vestry meeting is subdued. The deaths of Ephraim and Merith are like body blows to the life of the community. And this week we have to move our Sunday services into the parish hall for the rest of the year, which adds to our agitation. The earthquake retrofit of the church will start in a few weeks. The organ has been dismantled. The Community Kitchen will move out of the parish hall and downtown to Catholic Charities for the duration of the construction. The vestry views this as simple efficiency, and it is, but I privately grieve. In my heart, I know the possibility of the Kitchen's return, after the construction is over, is nearly nil. When everything is newly painted and the floors sanded and polished, who will want the men who spill salad, roll their bikes inside, and leave their smelly packs lying around? I feel, in Eastertide, as if everything is fragmenting, blowing apart.

Fund-raising for the retrofit is going well, reports the chair of the Capital Campaign Committee, but the construction company came in 39 percent over an earlier bid.

The program coordinator reports on plans for a fall workshop on human sexuality. In 1991 the General Convention of the Episcopal Church asked that each diocese hold parish workshops on sexuality, in an effort to educate and take a pulse. Trinity never got around to a workshop, and now seems like good timing.

Halfway through the meeting, Elly Wyatt asks to go into executive session. Turning to Kati Smith, she says, "Let's have the report of the ad hoc committee on . . ." She hesitates.

"Human sexuality," Mark says firmly. Then he laughs. "Specifically, mine."

"Right," Elly says.

Kati passes out a sheet of paper.

"These are the questions we think we as a vestry should think about, pray about, and discuss," she says. "Look them over and then let's set a date to get together and talk."

"Let's make sure we're all on the same page with this," Mark says. "These questions are meant to be the seeds for a frank discussion. We've hardly talked about this at all."

I read the list:

1. Do we want the Parish to know about Mark?
2. How to handle questions about Mark?
3. How does Mark date? Have a relationship? Have a partner?
4. How does a Vestry person make this ethical choice?
   a. Is gay lifestyle acceptable/unacceptable?
   b. Is this a social justice issue?
   c. How does a Vestry person decide?
   d. What are the Canonical ramifications of having a gay priest?
   e. What if you don't have an answer to 4a? What if you're unsure? How do you make a decision?
5. What does it mean for Trinity to be in the forefront on this issue?
6. Is there Parish support?
7. Are we going to lose members/$?
8. What impact on Capital Campaign/Stewardship?
9. Could this decision split the parish? and how will we handle it?
10. Does the Vestry want limitations on gay issues? Do we want this to be a gay parish?"

That about covers it, I think to myself.

"We meet with Anne Howard, the canon to the ordinary, in July," Elly says. "This is our last meeting with her, and it is our final mutual evaluation before we decide whether or not to call Mark as our rector."

"The committee suggests that we meet in August with a facilitator to go over these questions," Kati says. "In September, we'll have the workshop on human sexuality. At the work-shop, the vestry should be present and we should observe. Then, sometime after that, perhaps in October or November, we'll make our decision regarding Mark."

"Are there any questions?" Elly asks.

"I'm not sure we need to go through all of this," Elaine Christ says. "I mean, it seems like an awful lot."

"Well, Elaine," Steve says, "it's pretty serious."

"My concern," says Ed Potts, "is that we're in a 'we know something you don't know' position with the parish. How are we going to let them know?"

"I think we need to talk about all of this in August," Kati says. Plans are made for an August date. Judy Brown offers her house. Two facilitators are chosen: Robert Hagler, the prior at Mount Calvary, and Carol Bason, a respected local therapist. Throughout the conversation, I feel as if we are all together on a high wire, but also on the border of some large and inter-esting country where we will be changed simply by crossing into it.

I bring up a letter a parishioner has sent me. It's a com-plaint, listing in some detail various ways the vestry has let this person down. Mark appears to be irritated that I've brought it up.

"What did you want us to do with this?" he asks.

I flounder. I'm the new kid on the block and don't have much experience with vestry protocol.

"I'm not sure," I reply. "But I thought you needed to see it."

Various people make comments, clarify aspects of the letter they know something about, then fall silent. Finally Steve Gib-son comes to my rescue.

"I think Nora is smart enough to answer this," he says look-ing kindly at me. "You might suggest that if the person wants to address the whole vestry they can come to a meeting."

"Okay," I say, and gather up the copies of the letter. I sit there and a voice inside me says, They think you are a fool. I get more and more wrapped up in this feeling, my stomach feels tight and my chest hurts. Then suddenly out of nowhere I feel pierced by sweetness. And a powerful, not quite articulated sentence runs through my head: You can let this go. And I do. I feel just fine, but giddy, as if I've just awakened from sleep or stepped off a plane. I lighten up and look around. Down the table from me, I see that Kati has beautiful hands. The whole mood of the vestry lifts.

(When I tell the story to Ann Jaqua the next day, she says, "I've had that happen. A lot of grace during a small event, more grace than the event justifies. I think it may be that grace is always there but it gets through when we're not paying attention. I mean, it's there for bigger things but we don't see it. To apply it or remember it during bigger things or catch it then may take intentionality. In any case, you can live on that for a long time.")

During compline, Stephen chooses, among the four optional readings, the one from Jeremiah. "Lord, you are in the midst of us, and we are called by your Name: Do not forsake us, O Lord our God."

I WALK IN cold and wet to the soup kitchen, having been caught in a sudden, late rain. Two men are playing chess near the door. I spoon my soup standing at the serving table. It's good, very lemony. Little Alex asks me how I like my soup. I say I love it. He laughs. "Richard left me a note, to use the chicken stock a lady brought in. So I put in each of four bottles of the stock in each pot, stirred, added vegetables, rice, tasted it after thirty minutes, and—" He makes a spitting motion with his mouth. "It was lemonade. I had to go back over forty years of cooking experience to remember what to do."

"So what did you do?" I ask.

"Soy sauce," he replies.

I take a break and drive Alex downtown to the Broadway to buy him an umbrella. As we stand together in the elevator, Alex in his old blue jeans and torn jacket, I realize that for him the mall may as well be Mars. Afterward, he asks to be dropped off at the library.

"How come?" I ask.

"So I can look up recipes for the Kitchen," he replies. "And Juli meets me there. I'm teaching her Spanish."

Back at the Kitchen, Mike wants to talk. We stand in the hallway near the church office. He's now rail thin, his potbelly gone and with it all of his comforting manner. He's been showing up late to work, or not at all. Instead of his old cotton shirts and blue jeans, he's wearing a muscle T-shirt and tight bike shorts. I have never seen this before. How a man can be one person and then another in the space between Christmas and Easter? He speaks staccato: "My former wife, my former wife, has the court date. She's taking me to court."

Juli arrives from the library and we sit in the women's lounge to talk. We don't know what to do. Juli talks to Mike's girlfriend, who says, "He's under a lot of stress," and "He'll be all right." Meanwhile Mike rushes into the kitchen, grabs a piece of bread off a plate, shovels it into his mouth. I go back to the women's lounge and cry.

When I return to the dining room, Mark Asman is standing in his collar and shirtsleeves near the door into the dishwashing room. We stand together surveying the room. I congratulate him on using an inclusive prayer on Sunday: "In the name of the one God, Creator, Redeemer, Sanctifier," rather than, "Father, Son and Holy Spirit."

"Did it have anything to do with Anne Howard's presence in the congregation?" I ask. She was visiting, in her official capacity.

Mark laughs. "I'm not above politics, I'm afraid. May as well put it all out on the table." A woman is playing the piano and singing loudly. Just as Mark is saying, "May as well put it all out on the table," she joins us.

"Yes, that's what I say," she says. "Like my erotic parts, may as well let them show." We pause. She has a wonderfully crazy, open face.

She says, "Well, that's my repertoire, I can do evangelical songs and play the guitar." She's concentrating on Mark's face. He is looking impassive. "I can do other songs."

He says, "Thank you. However, we are restructuring the church right now and we can't make any plans until March." She looks at him. She looks through him. She nods, disappointed.

She says, "Well, okay, I'll be around," and she walks away.

"She saw right through that," Mark says.

"Yes, she did," I say.

I look at him, he looks at me.

"Well," he says, "it's all right that she saw right through that."

"Yes it is," I say. And then it's done. I feel a sense of reality expanding. To contain: a lie, a confession, and an assessment. One after the other. Like a chain.

That afternoon, I walk over to Cottage Hospital to visit Anne Howard, who had surgery the day before. She sleeps while I read. Mark arrives in his black suit and sits down heavily in another chair. Soon, the three of us are fast asleep. We wake, refreshed and startled, when a nurse comes in.

When I get home, I head toward my study to lie down. On the way, I push the button on our telephone answering machine. My brother's voice plays out. "Hi, Nora, it's Kit. I'm in the hospital. Presbyterian, room number 841. I can't find the phone number, call me up."

I get the number for the hospital from information, then

dial too fast and connect to a drunk person who sounds Greek. I try again and Kit answers.

"So, what's going on?"

"I don't know," he says slowly. "I couldn't shit for five days. I tried a bunch of laxatives. Nothing worked and I got worried, so Rande drove me up here. I saw Dr. Ortolano's partner and he put me in here. Dr. Ortolano's on vacation. They want to do X rays tomorrow. But I'm thinking I might just leave."

I feel a rush of panic. "You can't leave," I say. "You don't know what's wrong."

"Yeah," he says, quietly. "But you know, they don't, they probably won't know either. They've given me some stuff and they say that if my bowels move tomorrow morning or tonight, that's one thing. Some guy came in and said they might have to do surgery."

"What guy?"

"Dr. Maxwell. He's the surgeon on call, or maybe Dr. Ortolano's partner called him."

"Where is Rande?"

"She went home to feed the dogs."

"What will you do?"

"I'll stay the night, I think, but I'm not going to hang around while they do tests."

"You'll tell me as soon as you know?"

"Oh, yeah."

I go to my study, pick up the prayer book, and start to read psalms. "Have mercy on me, O Lord, for I am in trouble; my eye is consumed with sorrow," reads Psalm 31. ". . . Make your face to shine upon your servant, and in your loving kindness save me."

The next day, Kit calls early in the morning.

"Success," he says cheerfully.

"Well, now," I say. "Exactly what kind of success?"

"Let's not get clinical," he replies. "So I'm leaving. Packing up my bags. They want to do more tests, but I told them I had to get back to work."

After we hang up, I sit there in Vincent's study, watching the street outside. Two kids are riding new plastic tricycles in primary colors, red and blue. Across the street, our neighbor is standing on a ladder, trimming his hedge. Inside me a sort of river is flowing, filled with chunks of fear that fragment and collide.

I DROP BY the soup kitchen in the morning to pick up some forms to deliver to the city for a grant application. Today people look as if they might pass for "normal." They look fine until you get up close. I see my father's ruddy Irish face in Old Jack. An Asian woman wears white running shorts, tights, and a neon-green cap. She looks like a tourist until she sits down and takes off three shirts. Another woman has a chic haircut and wears an expensive leather jacket. With her mouth set in a grim line, I take her for a member of the Episcopal Church Women, but as she comes closer I see her briefcase is stuffed with bits of paper. They are a text, an ironic commentary on our lives.

I walk straight downtown to have lunch at a restaurant and I'm so used to the intimacy and lack of privacy among the poor and insane that I stare at everyone around me and receive a few glares in return. As I stare, I see some of what they try to hide; wounds surface.

Driving home later that night from a movie, our friend Jodie asks Vincent if he's a believer. No, he replies. She's leaning over from the backseat and she turns to me. "Do you think Vincent won't go to heaven?"

"No," I reply. "The God I believe in doesn't stand on technicalities."

"I believe in reincarnation," she says.

"If that's true, I'd like to come back as a tree," Vincent says.

I think of coming back as a tree, long limbs stretched to heaven, deep roots in the ground, birds in my hair.

"Do you believe in an afterlife?" Jodie asks.

"Yes," I say. "Something happened to Jesus, but I can't imagine what it will be like."

Then I remember an afternoon Jodie came over with other friends and we sat outside in the backyard.

"Do you remember that afternoon?" I ask Jodie. "When everything was so easy?"

"No," she says.

"It was sunny and everyone was relaxed, nothing special was going on. I was so glad to see you. I felt completely in the present. No part of me was missing. I think that has something to do with eternity."

"Yes," she says. "I know what you're talking about. I know exactly what you're talking about. I've had those moments, too."

AT THE END of May, Lois elects the surgery, because of an accident. Her feeding tube started working its way out of her stomach; by the next Saturday, she was in the hospital to put it back in. By Monday, she decided, because she was already in the hospital, she'd do the surgery.

On Wednesday evening, I'm making tomato sauce from early tomatoes at the farmers' market, feeling buoyant and ready for summer when the phone rings.

"Lois had surgery today," Ben says. "It took eight hours and they finally gave up. The surgeon told me he tried but he didn't have enough intestine to work with. They came to me and told me and he said he would try to work it out with plastic tubes and things and I said no, I didn't think Lois would want that."

"You had to make that decision alone?"

"I had help from the surgeon. The surgeon said he tries to remain objective but he couldn't in this case and he gave it a hundred and ten percent but it didn't work. So now what they are going to do is try to keep Lois comfortable."

On Monday, Memorial Day, I walk over to Cottage to see Lois. The hospital is becoming familiar terrain, an adjunct to the church. She's in a private room, sitting in a chair beside her bed with a tube up her nose and a bunch of IVs on poles near her head. Greta, her eldest daughter, is seated in front of Lois, removing pale nail polish from her hands. Sam is standing in a corner. Lois introduces me to Sam's girlfriend, Nicole, who is seated on the bed. Ralph, the eldest son, stands near the door. I hover next to him, not yet ready to walk into the room. Death is here and it repels me. I want to ward it off. Lois's face is gray, her legs swollen and yellow, her belly distended, but she is still elegant, her chin sharp, her bones high. "Sit down," she says, but I stand. The kids are all in various stages of nervous energy. Greta busily works on her nails, with cotton balls dipped in remover, talks about how she has heard that Nicole's father doesn't need more than four hours of sleep a night. "We have all been talking about how much sleep we need," Lois says to me. "My mother sleeps two hours at a stretch, then gets up and does things," Nicole says. She shifts uneasily on the bed.

"My mother was a model," she says. "She likes to have her feet done. She goes to a place where you sit in those rattan lounge chairs, like from Cost Plus, and they do your feet."

"Let's do that when I get out of here," Lois says to me. "Let's go and have our feet done and have a massage."

Nicole then talks about how she and Sam drove out from Boston and couldn't find a hotel room because it was Memorial Day weekend. "Flagstaff," she says, "We thought we'd find a room in Flagstaff." Ben walks in with a bunch of gardenias. When he puts them in the pot he brought from home, Lois says, "A creamer." They droop and so he removes them again and tries to put an elastic band around the stems; I reach forward and hold them so he can finish. "That's better," he says. Then he leaves the room.

Greta begins to polish her mother's nails. She talks about working for a florist and how she can't wear gloves because the work is too delicate. Over Christmas she got "florist's thumb."

"It turned brown and was infected and wouldn't go away and I couldn't work for a couple of days," she says, tracing a nail with a thin brush. Then she describes a dinner at her boss's house: "Seven courses, and it wasn't even a holiday. Salmon mousse and freshly shucked peas and roast beef." The others lean into her words. Lois looks distracted. When Ben returns, he has eaten downstairs; the others decide to go out and have lunch. It's two o'clock. As they leave, I move onto the bed. I let Lois know I don't plan to stay. I can't really tell whether I am of any help to her or if she feels she has to entertain me.

"Mark is a good visitor," she says.

"How is he a good visitor?" I ask.

"Well, for one thing, he visits," she says. "The priest I had before didn't like to visit people in the hospital. And for another, just before I went under this time, he snuck in and whispered a prayer in my ear."

I give her the base community's love and then lean over to hug her. She holds on tight with her thin, wiry arms and I hold on tight to her.

"And I like the oil Mark puts on my forehead," she says. "It smells of rosemary."

AT THE END of Eastertide, at the base community, Elizabeth says she was thinking of the base community the other day and called it "base camp."

"I thought about it for a while and it didn't seem so far off. Here we are, roped together at high altitude."

The Gospel we read tonight is from John, chapter thirteen. "I give you a new commandment," Jesus says, "that you love one another. By this everyone will know that you are my disciples, if you have love for one another."

"Yesterday, I brought Lois a bunch of roses," Mark Benson says.

"When I was in the hospital," Katrina says, "a doctor brought me clay to work with. I made an elephant. I was proud of it. It was the first thing I had been proud of in a long time."

I begin to tell them about my visit with Lois, my fears about Kit, my grief over Ephraim and Merith, and soon I'm crying and I can't stop.

"If you'd like to cry for a while, it's okay," Katrina says. "We can wait."

We are living in the shadow of the resurrection in community, I think; we are tasting and seeing.

"We leave the tomb, go out into the world, and are entrusted to be creators of a new work of transformation," Mark preached on Easter Sunday. "We never do it alone without our brothers and sisters, and we never do it alone because at the heart of every faith community is the heart of the resurrected Jesus."

I think of Mary Magdalene, Joanna, and Mary the mother of James, those whom Jesus befriended: the marginal, the outcast, the oppressed. And, not to forget, the hopeful. They stood in that tomb and endured its emptiness. Then they ran outside to tell the others. They gave all they had for something new.

Pentecost

EARLY ON A SUMMER morning two years ago, I was in my studio attempting to pray—that is, my eyes were closed and I was sitting on the floor. The swarm of thoughts that normally buzz through my mind when I am "praying" settled for a minute and left a wide open space. Into it came an image of a flame—more than an image; it was as if, near my right ear, a word was on fire. The next day I went to church and discovered it was Pentecost.

The Holy Spirit came to the Apostles, the story in the second chapter of Acts goes, in wind and flames. It was fifty days after Passover, fifty days after Easter. The disciples were together, "in one place."

"And suddenly from heaven there came a sound like a rush of a violent wind, and it filled the entire house where they were sitting. Divided tongues, as of fire, appeared among them, and a tongue rested on each of them. All of them were filled with the Holy Spirit and began to speak in other languages, as the Spirit gave them ability. . . . And at this sound the crowd gathered and was bewildered, because each one heard them speaking in the native language of each."

The third member of the Trinity arrives without warning and, unlike the youthful, dramatic son, moves in to stay. My friend Christina sees her sometimes as a little old lady who wades into a barroom brawl, shooting her six-guns into the air.

The story in Acts is the opposite of, a counterweight to, the story of the Tower of Babel, in which the builders of that ambitious tower suddenly spoke in foreign tongues and could not understand each other. In the Holy Spirit's arrival is the healing of Babel and the promise that we will all eventually understand each other not in our commonality, but in our individuality, in our diversity: "each . . . in the native language of each." We will all eventually understand each other, but in order to be understood, we must both speak and hear. In our speaking, our hearing, and our understanding, there will be half-measures, half-desires, misunderstandings, the turbulence of words.

IN THE GOSPEL READING for Pentecost Sunday, Jesus "breathes" on the disciples and says to them, "Receive the Holy Spirit." He follows that immediately with the heart of the matter: "If you forgive the sins of any, they are forgiven. If you retain the sins of any, they are retained."

"How are you doing about forgiveness?" asks the Reverend Canon Lauren Artress in her sermon at Trinity on Pentecost Sunday this year. "How is it coming along?" She stands behind the podium in the parish hall, a modest woman with short graying hair and an alert, wry face, looking out at a congregation seated on newly acquired plastic chairs. At Grace Cathedral in San Francisco she is responsible for "bridging ministries," creative ways of connecting the Church with the outer world and vice versa. She is our guest today, to preach and bless our newly made labyrinth, a huge canvas burrito that lies folded on a counter in the dishwasher room.

In 1991, Artress copied a circular pattern from the floor of Chartres Cathedral in France and painted it on a forty-two-foot-wide piece of canvas. The pattern, called a labyrinth, has eleven rings and a six-petaled flower in its center. The difference between it and a maze is that a labyrinth is one continuous path, folded in on itself and very baffling, but without tricks, blind alleys, or false leads. You enter the Chartres labyrinth at a break in the outer ring and follow the path in front of you. After about a third of a mile, you find yourself in the center.

The labyrinth at Chartres was laid in the floor of the cathedral some time between 1194 and 1220, during the time of Chartres' first architect, a person who went by the pseudonym Scarlet. It was not clear who designed it, why exactly it was made, or how it was used, although there are hints and rumors that labyrinths were walked as the last stretch of a pilgrimage. And, while the one at Chartres is among the most sophisticated, there were hundreds of labyrinths in Europe during the Middle Ages. At the cathedral at Amiens there is a handsome octagonal labyrinth, a black path set in green marble. At St. Lucca Cathedral in San Martino, Italy, there is a small labyrinth set into a wall, worn from the many hands that have traced it. Greece has a simpler, seven-circuit labyrinth on Crete; Ireland has labyrinths carved onto the doorknobs of churches; England has labyrinths dug into sod.

Canon Artress laid hers down in the nave at Grace on New Year's Eve in 1991 and offered it to people to walk. The wait that night was six hours long.

"The labyrinth is a wonderful bridging tool because you can walk it no matter what tradition you're coming from," said Artress in a magazine interview. "It's a container. You can literally walk into it and because it has boundaries and because it has a beginning and an end, you can walk into a whole other world that's set aside as a spiritual place."

"Today, we've lost touch with such tools, tools that once formed the heart of Christian spiritual practice," she said in a second interview. "Christianity teaches that we should love our enemies, but fails to outline the steps required to evolve that capacity. The Church has taught us what to believe but not how to believe—how to connect our faith with our daily lives."

Today, as she preaches, her tone is gentle, empathic. "Anyone inside that you hold with a grudging heart? That is often a question I take into the labyrinth with me. Am I holding anger against someone? Who do I have a hard heart toward? As Christians, we need to know how to let the love of God into our hearts. How do we open our hearts to the Holy Spirit who longs to weave us together into community?"

LAST JUNE AT Trinity we borrowed a small canvas labyrinth from a troupe of liturgical dancers in Berkeley and placed it in the back of the church for a week. The idea of a "spiritual tool," something that might help us pray, clear a space, was new and wonderful. None of us had ever heard that Christianity had any such tradition.

The Berkeley labyrinth had narrow paths and was stained with wax from votive candles, but as I watched the men and women walking it, I felt I watched a slow, changing dance. When each person came off the labyrinth, I found myself involuntarily bowing to him or her, as Buddhists bow to the spirit in one another. Soon, we were talking about making our own. We figured it would take about ten of us a month to make one thirty feet by thirty feet, a perfect size for the guild hall, a room adjacent to the parish hall. (A labyrinth that would fit in the back of the church was too small.) But the canvas alone would cost at least eight hundred dollars, and we had no idea, actually, how much time or how many people it would take.

"Humor me," said Mark Asman, as I fretted early this year. "Make a decision."

Finally, Carolyn Alevra, who had originally brought news

of the labyrinth to Trinity, donated the funds in memory of her brother-in-law. Allison Jaqua volunteered to head the team, and she found a woman who had inherited her father's sailmaking business. Yes, the woman said, she could sew something that big. One Saturday morning in early May, Iva Schatz and I sat on the polished floor of the dance studio at Westmont College with a clean pale canvas stretched out before us and tried to remember the formula for the circumference of a circle.

We worked on the labyrinth in the evenings and on Saturdays. With help from a kit we bought from Grace, we drew eleven concentric rings using a broomstick, a piece of string, and a carpenter's pencil, then erased parts of the rings to form the turns. Women lay on their stomachs, erasing, for hours— we did not know when we started how well cotton canvas absorbs graphite. While they erased, the women talked about their former marriages (with emphasis on their ex-husbands' affairs), their time-consuming and often treasured jobs, their beloved children. Others came and went, carrying in supplies: pizza, new erasers, knee pads. The work had a quality of an unfolding, ongoing story—we laughed a lot—and my discipline became not to crack the whip to get things done but to let the work unfold and the women reveal themselves to one another, in a finely tuned give-and-take. Watch and wait, I told myself, watch and wait. This was the work of the Holy Spirit, I saw later, two birds with one stone.

The day we chose the paint color, Mark, Allison, and I drove downtown and stood around a counter while the owner of the paint store mixed purple and blue. Mark, in mufti, got bored and began shooting baskets with a foam Nerf ball. As he failed for the fifth time, Allison said quietly, "Don't quit your day job."

A week before Pentecost Sunday, we laid the canvas down

in the guild hall and, night after night, Allison; Anne Roediger, a nurse; Betty Bickel; and a small select team painted over the pencil lines with inch-wide foam wheels dipped in labyrinth blue. On Friday night, not a moment too soon, they finished. The image I had of our labyrinth then, and still hold, was of a large, sleeping dragon. The great rings lay under the old lights in the guild hall in lively readiness.

CELTIC MONKS OF the sixth century set sail from Ireland and Wales in small boats made of hides, reports Esther de Waal, to drift without oars until they found land. They wandered from Iceland to Italy seeking their true home, in perpetual travel, *peregrinati,* pilgrims, or as St. Columbanus called all Christians, "guests of the world."

"Pilgrims are persons in motion—passing through territories not their own," writes Richard Niebuhr, "seeking something we might call completion, or perhaps the word clarity will do as well, a goal to which only the spirit's compass points the way." Before the day of Pentecost, before that crowded moment in Jerusalem, the disciples were in hiding or had returned to their old lives. On Pentecost, they became the first pilgrims. With those flames riding their ears, they got into boats or walked out into the countryside to carry their words to the ends of the earth.

This is the craving of the Holy Spirit, the driving passionate voice. It is her hand set against my back, I see now. It is not finished, she whispers. It did not end with the one on the cross.

AFTER THE SERVICE on Pentecost Sunday we lift the new labyrinth from the kitchen counter and unfold it in the guild hall. Elizabeth Reifel brought potted green plants to place at the edges. Anne Roediger has made a ring of flowers for the wrought-iron candle stand. Lauren Artress says a blessing:

"May the Gracious God, who, by the Holy Spirit, caused many tongues to proclaim Jesus as Lord, strengthen our faith as we walk the path of life. We ask that you guide our turnings, correct our errors, support us when we falter, and guide us to love and compassion for you, for ourselves, and for others, especially those who differ from us."

Many members of the parish line up to walk the labyrinth. I want to say to them, You are throwing yourselves into a boat. On the edge of the canvas sit rows of empty shoes. Says one woman after her walk, "It was the best meditation for me. Much better than trying to sit and pray."

"When I finished walking, I realized I had a hole in my sock," Steve Gibson says. "I think there are labyrinth people and there are nonlabyrinth people. I am not a labyrinth person."

"What is this?" Martha Smith, from the Altar Guild, asks Mark.

"Why don't you give it a try?" he replies.

For the next several weeks, it seems we walk it all the time. One evening, we walk it in near darkness. Mark Asman, halfway through, suddenly lifts his hands in the gesture of a priest at prayer. Later he says, "I couldn't stop them. Nothing had happened to me before on the labyrinth and I was just about to give it up."

Martha Smith shows up one evening and walks it. She comes back the next night.

Before I walked it the first time, I felt foolish. It is very silly, a large part of me said, to walk around in circles on a piece of ten-gauge canvas. One step in, however, and it was like setting foot on a distant planet. The science fiction novels about gates to other worlds apply here, to this odd shape on the floor.

Right after Pentecost, I am walking in the evening. The old leaded-glass windows are tipped open, the fireplace is like the mouth of a cave, the door to the kitchen is ajar. As I walk, I suddenly see other doors on the old paneled wall near the fireplace, doors where there are no doors, and am so frightened by this near hallucination, I draw back. But in this container a great calm presides. There are other doors, I see, many of them. And then, just as I pass a window, a breeze wafts in, the lightest touch of breath, a gift beautiful, tender, and sufficient.

I ASK BEN HITZ how Lois is doing and he replies, "Drifting."

On the Friday after Pentecost, I go to see her. She is lying on a gray love seat in her bedroom, looking out at the lavender in her garden. Her expression, like that of my friend Ben before he died, is detached, almost cold, vaguely irritated. She sucks ice cubes and slips cranberry juice into her mouth. She should spit out the juice into a little pink hospital plastic tray because she isn't supposed to swallow, but she easily confuses the glass and the tray, and sometimes drinks from the tray and spits into the glass. Then, with a mischievous look on her face, she swallows. Ben, coming in, notices.

"Spit it out, Lois," he says and then to me, sotto voce: "I don't know what to do about that." And then to himself, "I don't know what to do about that."

"What are you thinking about, Lois?" I ask, hoping she'll say, "Death," and then I'll know what the ground rules are.

"I don't know," she parlays. "What are you thinking about?"

Chicken-hearted, I lie. "The labyrinth."

"I hear it's pretty," she says. "What a project for you, Nora."

It is like her to think of me, even now.

"The base community sends their love," I say.

"I'll be back there," she says, in a settled tone. "I'll be back in that community." I remind her of the mushroom-hunt story she told us. She smiles. Then I tell her I want to plant a garden at Trinity, in the planters outside the guild hall.

"It's a western-facing garden," I say. "What should I plant there?"

"I tell you what," she replies, looking straight at me. "You plant mushrooms on the west side. And I'll plant something on the other side."

She pauses, and then goes on, "And I will tell you what comes up. I've never planted on the other side."

THE KITCHEN IS now located in the heart of downtown at Catholic Charities, a smaller space, but friendly and clean. It is a temporary location, we tell ourselves, only until we are done with the earthquake retrofit at Trinity. Today, Ann Jaqua and I sit down to eat macaroni and cheese with spinach salad and chopped jicama. We're just getting into it when Faustino brings over a small, round woman—all smiles. Faustino introduces her in Spanish. She greets me in Spanish and I get that her name is Yolanda. I see she has an employment application in her hands. My heart expands. An employment application. I can do this; it will be simple. We fill out her name, last name first, first name last. The date. Her address. *"La dirección?"* I ask. *"La ciudad?"* Is she over eighteen years old? I can't remember the Spanish word for "eighteen" so I just fill in, "Yes."

"Are you a citizen or do you have resident alien status?" She pulls out her Resident Alien card and I write in "Yes." Then we get to "What position are you applying for?" and my Spanish runs out. Faustino comes over. He can't read English. He calls to a man in a red shirt eating lunch, whom I vaguely remember as having gone to Mexico. The man comes over and translates what type of job: *"Qué tipo de trabajo?"* he asks

Yolanda, and gets a blank look. They do better on the school part. She completed fifth grade, he says, and together we make up things she studied: math, science, grammar. Then he asks her, out of the blue, if she studied psychology. She laughs and says no, and I remember that this man is also just a wee bit crazy. Here we are, a woman who speaks very little Spanish, a woman who speaks no English, and a man who speaks English and pretty good Spanish but who happens to be nuts. Here we are together, *peregrinati,* guests of the world.

Somehow we get through it. We make up references: Richard, the cook, will be one, and I will be one, too, and her sister whose married name is at least different from hers. We find out, through the translation work of the guy in the red shirt, that under "Activities or Special Skills" we can write "Basketball."

She says she lives with her *hermano* and his wife and their six children in Goleta and I make a cramped expression with my hands and she nods. Later she says, "In English, *como se dice 'hermano'*?"

"Brother," I say.

"Brewsher."

"Brother."

"Brewther."

"Brother."

"Broother."

"Bueno."

I slap my hand on the table. "*Mesa es* table."

"Tamble."

"Table."

"Table."

"Bueno."

I walk across the courtyard to the Catholic Charities office and make three copies of the employment application and bring them back to her, and she laughs and throws her arms around me and says, "Thanks, lady." And I laugh. At her exuberance, at how far she has to go.

The next week, the Kitchen is quiet. Three servers on the line are from the Church of Latter-Day Saints. The soup is yellow squash and the salad has sections of oranges in it. For dessert, cinnamon bread with icing.

Yolanda comes into the kitchen carrying a letter, her face has expectation written all over it. She hands the letter to me. It has a business feel to it and I open it. "Thank you for your résumé," it reads. "We have no positions open at this time." I look at her, all full of hope, and I shake my head and say, *"No trabajo."* Her face falls. All the light goes out of it. She says, *"Gracias. Voy a comer,"* and slides out of the kitchen, toward the serving line.

Peter comes out of the dishwasher room and points out some squash Faustino has baked and buttered. "Eat some," he says. "It's good."

Outside, at the bus table, I'm wiping down trays when a woman comes over. She's breathing so much alcohol I look around to make sure no one lights a match. She offers to help and I think, Oh, well, why not and say yes, she can help wipe down trays. She walks around to my side of the table, wipes down a tray from the top of the stack and then moves the whole stack to her right. I point out that each tray needs to be wiped down. Oh, she says amiably, and starts wiping down each one, fast, with real savoir-faire. Then she picks the whole stack up and starts to carry them over to the serving table.

"No," I say, "we have to count them."

"Count them?" she replies as if she's in a loony bin, but she goes along with it.

"My son is in Florida," she says. "He's been straight for three years. I'm going to leave on Sunday to go live with him. Life is too hard on the streets."

"What is it like?"

"It's cold. And"—she makes a nervous, floating gesture with her hand—"everyone acts as if they don't like you. And a bath. Oh, a bath. I had one yesterday and washed my hair. If I hadn't, I'd look even worse." She peers at me. "You've never lived on the streets, have you?"

As we are closing down, Peter comes over to me and says, "There's a man out there who is blessing everything in sight and won't leave." I go out. A man is sitting at the table, making cross motions with his hands. I say hello. He motions. I say, "Hello. I'm sorry, but the kitchen is closed now."

"Oh," he says. "Do you want a recipe?" He hands me a napkin on which is written, "noodle! Veg! Cheese! Meat CAS-SAROLE." It resembles a painting by "Wölfli" or one of the other painters from psychiatric hospitals: it has a huge amount of life stuffed into nonsense. He has drawn a pan on a stove. His drawings are good. "One Pan! i lb MACCARONI, 2 cans med #8 can cream of mushroom soup, i pkg. frozen mixed vege. (opt. 4) cheese!? (opt. 5) tuna!? chicken (ask first!) may prepare sans meat and or add 'meat' in separate saucepan for everyday." A smaller drawing of a saucepan. Then, "NOT thicker noodle. Use your brain! Brown meat, prepare noodles (boil!) and drain partially. Add vege. soup and water low heat warm, keeps well in refr. microwave able, reheatable. Take to work etc." A drawing of a bowl. "try noodles, hamburger, meatballs with salt and pepper stroganoff."

"Thank you. I'll show Richard, our cook," I say.

He says, "Do you have a minute?"

"No, I don't. I have to be somewhere at two."

He stands up.

"What's your name?" I ask.

"Are you a doctor?" he replies.

"No. I'm a volunteer. My name is Nora."

He says a name I can't understand, we shake hands, and he leaves.

THE NEXT DAY, June 14, my afternoon is tight: a haircut at one-thirty, then to the Kitchen to meet with Mike, then over to visit Lois. Mike seems to have broken down completely; he doesn't show up for work. Juli and I must fire him and also tell him he cannot come to the Kitchen at all for the space of a month. We've figured out that we can hire his girlfriend to clean in his place, thus making sure that they don't lose what income they have.

When I get there, Mike is standing outside the door with Juli. He rambles about his court date. Juli offers to go with him to court.

"Mike," I say, "I have to ask you not to come to the Kitchen for a month, starting today. We've talked to you about the quality of your work, and being on time, but nothing has changed."

"I'm just having trouble," he says.

"I know," I say.

"Is there anything we can do for you?" Juli asks.

"You could lend me some money to go to Oakland," he says. "My brother threw me out of their house. I can go up there to see my father."

"I'll think about that," Juli says.

"I want to see my father," Mike says.

We stand there, the three of us. I look down at my empty hands.

"Could I have some food today?" Mike says.

"Of course," Juli says. She turns and goes into the kitchen and brings out bread, some cheese, and an apple.

"Thank you," Mike says, and turns and walks away.

I drop by the house to pick some flowers for Lois. Rachel has left a message on the machine to call the church office. When I call, she says, "Lois Hitz died an hour ago."

My knees give and I sit down fast on the bed. Other parts of me tell me they can sustain or absorb this information, but my knees don't lie.

Finally I go outside to pick roses, coreopsis, poppies, Canterbury bells, Mexican sage. The flowers she liked, wild arrangements.

Ben is coming out of the house when I arrive. He says, "Nora, do you know?" I say yes.

Inside, it's quiet and clean. Mark Asman is standing in the kitchen leaning on the tiled counter. He nods as I come in. I go into the bedroom. Lois is lying in a twin hospital bed next to their double bed. Her neck and chest are arched forward, her mouth and eyes open. Her skin is stretched tight over the bones of her body. A catheter hangs from her chest. I brush her hair and smooth her forehead with my hand and say to her what comes into my mind, which is little more than "Oh, Lois."

Dee and the boys are in the garden. Dee, in a blue sweater, looks brave and strong, a hundred times stronger than the young woman standing by her mother's bed only a month ago. The boys look lost. In the kitchen, Ben talks about how he prayed for this all day because it had been so hard, she had suffered so much, the incision from the surgery had not drained properly, the colostomy bag leaked, the hospice nurses deserve, he says sadly, "hardly more than a C+."

"I was blessed," he says finally. "I was married to her for thirty-eight years." Mark and I lean toward him. We are waiting with him for the hospice nurse to come, and then the funeral home.

"Where did you meet her?" I ask.

"In London. Lois loved to tell that story. She said we met in Kew Gardens, but I don't think we did, I think she just liked to tell it that way. Anyway, we met, we were both from Indianapolis. Nothing much happened. Then we met again, a couple of months later, back home, and we got engaged.

"Wait," he says. "I have something to show you." He leaves the room and then returns with a manila folder marked "Family Photos." From it he pulls a black-and-white picture of Lois when she was twenty-three. Her high cheekbones, arched eyebrows, a sculpted, powerful face. "She was so beautiful, Ben," I say.

"Well," he replies, "she didn't always look this good, but she was pretty." Then he adds, "She was as wise and as good as she was beautiful."

The nurse finally comes, and she and Dee take out the catheter. When they are finished, the nurse calls the mortuary. They come in minutes, a man and a woman, in suits. They explain to Ben what they will do.

"Have you removed the jewelry from her?" they ask.

Ben goes the bathroom, gets some oil, and puts it on his hand. He takes her left hand in his and removes a white-gold band, and then a white-gold ring set with a dark blue stone and diamonds. One thin gold band remains. He tries to pull it off but cannot.

"Nora, you try," he says and I try but can't.

The young man from the mortuary tries as well, but fails.

"Is this her wedding band, Ben?" Mark asks.

"Yes," Ben replies. "I don't think she ever took it off."

"Why not leave it on," Mark says gently. Ben bows his head, then nods.

"You may not want to watch us take her from the bed," the woman says. One by one we leave the room, leaving Dee as the last. She leans down and kisses her mother on the forehead.

LOIS'S REQUIEM EUCHARIST follows three days later, on Saturday, in the parish hall. The room is packed, not only with Lois's friends and family but with people from the parish.

This is the community of faith, different from family and friends, but feeling so keenly the loss of one, "a sheep of thine own fold," as the old prayer goes, "a lamb of thine own flock." An elderly woman says to me, "I just wanted to be here. I liked seeing her on Sunday. She was a part of us."

I haven't cried since Rachel told me on the phone, but when we get to the last stanzas of the opening hymn, "St. Patrick's Breastplate," a great song of battle and praise with words by Patrick himself, then I weep with the others.

"I bind unto myself today the virtues of the starlit heaven," we sing together. "The glorious sun's life-giving ray, the whiteness of the moon at even." Dee, Greta, and their brothers stand with their father in a row of dark suits and faces chalked white. "The flashing of the lightning free, the whirling wind's tempestuous shocks, the stable earth, the deep salt sea, around the old eternal rocks."

I think of Lois gone fully back into the wind, the deep salt sea, the eternal rocks, no longer a guest but a wedded branch, a limb. I think of her now "on the other side" planting what is planted there. At the base community on Thursday night, a day after Lois's death, Dodie Little said, "She savored every day. And we were the beneficiaries of that savoring. In her stories that she was generous enough to share with us, we got a glimpse of how eternity is giving oneself fully to the moment, by filling that moment up."

Elizabeth Reifel said that when she heard that Lois had died, she lay down on her bed and thought about her. "It was a complete thought," she said. "Lois had nothing missing."

The priest at her former parish, Connor Lynn, rises to give the eulogy. He tells a story. Lois told him it was time the parish began composting its garbage. The two of them decided that they would buy a worm bin. The worms arrived, Lynn says, and he carefully followed all the directions, but weeks later, it became apparent that something had gone wrong; the garbage remained more or less intact.

"I was afraid to tell Lois," he says "but finally she discovered it. I told her I was afraid I just wasn't up to the task. She replied, 'It's all right, Connor; neither were the worms.' "

Her ashes stand on the altar in a rosewood urn carved in the last few days by a man who had made furniture for her and Ben. He called Ben on Thursday and brought it over this morning.

At the end we sing, "Abide with me! Fast falls the eventide; / The darkness deepens: Lord, with me abide! . . ." and then move into the guild hall to eat a feast the Hitz children have prepared: fresh tomatoes with basil and olive oil, a red-onion tart, and an apricot cobbler. When I leave, they are sitting in a circle of chairs with friends, plates on their knees.

That afternoon I think about how I miss her face, her voice, the touch of her strong hand. Our comfort as creatures is in the body, the warmth of flesh. This is what we count on, what arms and heartens us. And this is the very thing that is impermanent, that is taken away. I say to God, This is unnecessarily cruel.

St. Augustine wrote, "It is solved by walking."

In late June, I drive to Berkeley to visit Cynthia and decide one afternoon to walk the labyrinth at Grace Cathedral. The cathedral is still and almost empty, the labyrinth laid out at the back near the baptismal font, its paths marked in purple. As I enter the labyrinth I see a verger dressed in long purple robes standing near its outer edge talking to a man in tweeds and a small woman dressing one of the smaller altars with luxuriant white flowers.

As I walk, they come into view, then vanish. A choir is

singing in French at the high altar. A chart at the back of the church announces that Grace has reached the thirteen-million-dollar mark in its capital campaign. All this becomes a tableau, like one of Brueghel's paintings, lives frozen, varied, packed together—the children skating on a pond, the plowman in the field, Icarus falling from the sky—the animation so close to the surface in the paintings they almost burst into life. The woman's hands arranging the flowers; the beautiful French voices; the folds of the verger's purple robes and his false, cheerful voice; the red-marked thermometer of the money chart—each one comes into view as I sweep the circles of the labyrinth.

At one point, as I walk an outer ring, I feel the whole thing moving as a disk, turning in space, a huge flat globe. And when I arrive at the center, what catches and holds my eye? The ultimate scene: the one on the cross, hanging, far away, "Forsaken," as the Leonard Cohen song goes, "almost human."

That evening, Cynthia suggests we go on an early-morning hike. She has something to show me.

We get up early in a Bay Area fog and drive up to a small parking lot in the hills. From there, we walk up a trail along the edge of a hill, and then through oak trees. The fog is moving in wisps through the trees. I can hear Cynthia's breathing as we walk.

We come around the side of the hill, and the landscape opens up: we can see the rounded tops of rolling hills, with brown grasses on them. We walk a little way and then come to an abrupt edge.

"Look down," Cynthia says.

I do. Below me is a pond with reeds growing at its sides. A few ducks sit on the water. Next to the pond is a labyrinth.

It is cut into the dirt, and the paths are marked with low walls of stones. Its design is simpler than the one at Chartres; it's a copy of the oldest labyrinth pattern known, seven paths, from Crete—famous for the legend of Theseus and the Minotaur.

Cynthia and I climb down a steep hillside and walk in. People's feet have deepened the paths into grooves between the stones. The wind brushes the reeds on the pond. She grins and walks, fast, toward the center. I follow her, somewhat more slowly, trying to get the feel of this new labyrinth. I like the uneven ground and the stones, but it's also littered and kind of funky. When we get to the center, there is a low stone on which people have placed little offerings: a penny, a piece of a tarot card, a faded flower, a button. Cynthia is dismayed that we have nothing to leave; I pull a cough drop wrapper out of my pocket, and we secure it with a little stone.

"Well, I say a little prayer to whoever," Cynthia says loudly, and I offer one to the Holy Spirit to look out for my tough friend. We walk out.

Almost a month later, in the middle of one of our conversations on the phone, Cynthia says, "I've decided that when the time comes, I want my ashes scattered at the labyrinth in the hills. Will you see to it?"

"Yes," I reply.

CHRISTIANS OF THE MIDDLE AGES made one binding commitment to the church: that they would, at some time in their lives, make a pilgrimage if not to Jerusalem at least to Rome. Pilgrimage was a vast combination of intents, purposes, and motives. From it emerged the idea of travel as a changing experience, even a psychological necessity. Maps for pilgrims were the first travel guides. According to J. G. Davies in *Pilgrimage Yesterday and Today*, a tenth-century manuscript (which probably contains material from the fifth and even the fourth centuries), the "Itinerarium Salisburgense," describes how to find one's way through the holy city (Rome), the locations of its major shrines, and whether they are above or below ground.

The travel itself was hard going. In 1139, it took forty-nine days to reach Rome from Canterbury. French diaries reported the deaths of eleven out of twenty pilgrims from exhaustion on one trip to the Holy Land. Bandits attacked the unarmed pilgrims; inns and other accommodations were few and far between.

Various corruptions of the strictly ascetic pilgrimage appear to have been present almost from the beginning: "Vigils . . . were often not devoted to spiritual exercises," writes Davies, "but to sleeping, to idle conversation, to the consumption of picnics, to the singing of popular ballads or the playing of musical instruments." Ladies were said to find a pilgrimage a convenient (and virtuous) method of arranging a rendezvous with their lovers.

The collecting of relics became the focus of so many pilgrimages that in the *Decameron* Boccaccio had his Brother Cipolla (Brother Onion) return from Jerusalem with these items: a bottle containing the noise of the bells of Solomon's temple and one of the feathers dropped by the Archangel Gabriel when he appeared to the Virgin Mary in Nazareth.

By the sixteenth century, the gathering of relics and the granting of indulgences had become so central to pilgrimage that Martin Luther, in 1519, announced: "All pilgrimages should be stopped. There is no good in them."

Even in the midst of corruption and mixed motives, however, pilgrimage contained the seed of a hidden truth about faith. Seen through our modern eyes, the lives of saints and pilgrims seem excessive, bordering on the crazed: Joan and her voices, Francis and his kiss upon the leper's lips, Julian of Norwich nearly walled into a cell, bands of pilgrims walking barefoot toward a shrine. Excess marks the lives of saints and pilgrims. Viewed through the lens of faith, however, these lives reveal this truth: the love of God for us is excessive and deserves, even demands, extravagance in return.

IN MIDSUMMER SANTA BARBARA pays for its temperate winters by enduring a dense fog that gathers in the morning, lifts briefly in the afternoon, then returns, colder, at night. The night of the vestry meeting, in mid-July, is an exception—it's actually warm. I wear a light dress and feel the way I felt as a child in summer, as if I had all the time in the world. Tonight we meet with Anne Howard, in her role as canon to the ordinary, to go over the final "Mutual Ministry Review," a discussion of how Mark is doing as priest-in-charge, how we are doing as a vestry, and how the congregation is doing in relation to both parties. The congregation has completed a "parish profile," a series of questions regarding life at Trinity including "What I like most about Trinity" and "What Trinity's strengths are" and "What I like least." As a vestry, we've been given a set of questions to think over at this meeting: What is there to celebrate? Have there been any surprises? Are there any conflicts?

If this final review goes well—we have completed two others—we will almost certainly call Mark as our rector sometime in the fall, after the Human Sexuality Workshop. Our hope is that the workshop will give us a sense of how the congregation, or at least how a good percentage of the congregation, feels about sexuality in general and homosexuality in particular. We need to find out if there is grave conflict over homosexuality or just confusion or something in between. And when and how to tell the congregation "about Mark," as we have begun to phrase it? How to "get everyone on the same page" without destroying Mark's privacy and making a circus out of it? We still don't know. That, too, we'll talk about in August. What has become apparent as we get closer to the workshop is that we are doing it as much for Mark's sake as for our own.

"I think he wants to know that everyone in the parish is comfortable with homosexuality before we call him," Elly Wyatt said early in the week. "I'm not sure we're *ever* going to get that kind of affirmation."

Planned for tonight is an executive session (at seven-twenty p.m., on the precise agenda) with "The Reverend Canon Anne Howard," who arrives in black shirt, collar, and scarlet blazer. At seven-twenty-five, Anne takes the chair. She begins by reminding us that the ministry review is a "three-way evaluation," of Mark, of the congregation, and of the vestry. Then we make our way through the questions. We know from the profile that many persons in the congregation rate Mark as "What I like most about Trinity" and include him in their list of "What Trinity's strengths are." People have told the vestry how comfortable they feel with him as a priest, as a pastoral counselor, and as a confessor. Tonight, various people on the vestry report that they like to work with Mark, that his leadership style is "participatory" but also "take-charge." The capital campaign is highly successful, and new people are streaming through the doors.

"Is there anything in the canons of the church that prohibits us from calling a gay priest?" asks Steve.

Anne pulls from her sheaf of papers a blue book, the *Canons of the Episcopal Church*, opens it, and reads: "All Bishops of Dioceses and other Clergy shall make provisions to identify fit persons for Holy Orders and encourage them to present themselves for Postulancy. No one shall be denied access to the selection process for ordination in this Church because of race, color, ethnic origin, sex, national origin, marital status, sexual orientation, disabilities or age, except as otherwise specified by these Canons."*

"Well, that's clear," Steve says.

"Is there anything else?" Anne asks.

No one has anything more to say.

"So," Anne says, "what are you going to do next?"

"We're going to meet in August," Kati says, "and talk about the issue of human sexuality. Then, I guess, if everything goes well, we'll call Mark. I mean, why not?"

"Why are we waiting until after that meeting in August?" Steve asks.

At this, Mark's face tightens. He looks quickly at his papers.

"Because," I say, looking over at Mark, "we need to talk over as a vestry how we feel about all this and then get a read of the congregation during the Human Sexuality Workshop."

"The whole process has been based on Mark wanting to wait until October, until after the workshop," Stefani adds.

"But we know how we feel now. What's going to change?" pipes in the normally quiet Elaine Christ.

"Yes," Anne agrees. "I think you do."

Mark squirms, but doesn't say anything.

"What are we going to learn that we don't already know?" Steve says, turning to Mark. "And, frankly, I think it's better to have you as the rector as we go into the workshop. I want to do these workshops, I want to go through this process, I want to participate, and I want to do it *with* my rector."

"But we did say we should wait until the fall," Kati says, uncertain.

---

*Anne read Canon 4, from Title III, Section 1 of the church canons, the only canon that mentions sexual orientation. She did not read the last line of the canon: "No right of ordination is hereby established." This "warning," or a version of it, is attached to many documents regarding entry into the ordination process, to prevent persons from believing that, should they enter the long road toward ordination, they will automatically come out the other end ordained.

"Can you tell me again why you wanted to do that?" Anne asks.

"Because," says Stefani, her voice close to breaking. "That's what Mark wants, or wanted."

"Why are you wedded to this time line, Mark?" Anne asks.

The room is full of something I can't put my hand on. Something animated, alive, is moving in it. Stefani is near tears. Steve is quiet, watchful. Anne looks expectant. Mark is not happy. I want to find a way to stop this, to give him some room, but whatever it is, it's moving too quickly for me to grasp. A door is closing, another one is opening. Now I see why they called it wind, a great rushing power.

"I'd like to put a motion on the table," Elaine says.

Everyone turns toward her.

"I'd like to move we call Mark as our rector."

Steve starts to speak, but Mark interrupts him. "We're not in a formal vestry session," he says. "It is not appropriate to make a motion."

Elaine's eyebrows shoot up.

"You're not chairing this session," she says. "Anne is."

"That is correct, Elaine," Anne says. "I am chairing this session."

The color has drained from Mark's face. I look at Anne. She smiles at me, and shakes her head, Whew.

"I want to make a motion," Elaine begins, but Mark interrupts again.

"I have got to have some time," he says. "I have got to have ten minutes to myself."

"You've got it," Anne says quickly. "Shall we take a break? I'd say, fifteen minutes. Then we'll come back. Okay, Mark?"

"Okay," he says and stands up, looks around the room, then goes into his office and closes the door.

Anne and I walk outside. In silence, we walk up the sidewalk and then down the block, toward the street corner. We walk fast without speaking for a few minutes.

"I think this is the Holy Spirit," she finally says. "It feels like all we have to do is get out of the way. I don't think I've ever seen anything like this before. At least," she says firmly, "not at a vestry meeting."

I nod. I feel as if I'm trying to regain my footing.

The others are wandering around, outside on the sidewalk and inside in the hall. In the air is expectation and a kind of giddy excitement. Elly says, "I guess he's praying in there. I know I'm praying. I have no trouble praying on my feet."

Anne calls us together and we walk inside. Mark's chair is empty and his office door is still closed. Once most of us are seated, he opens the door and walks in. And, as Stefani said later, "Something powerful and prayerful came in with him."

In the presence of what came into the room with Mark, all that has been giddy and full floats to the ground. He sits down into a silence that is like a wide, flat lake. He looks at his folded hands. Finally he smooths the papers in front of him and says, "I've just realized that I have my own homophobia. I don't really believe that you want me." He stops, then continues. "I have been so used to being unacceptable all my life, that I still can't believe that I am accepted by you. I don't believe," he says ruefully, "that you'll still love me in the morning."

Stefani pushes back her tears with the heel of her hand.

"Oh, come on, Mark," Steve says. "We wanted you after we found out about your Myers Briggs."

"I'd like to put on the table a motion I made a while ago," Elaine says. "Which was so rudely put off the table"—she grins at Mark—"by someone who wasn't even the chair at the time. I'd like to move that we call Mark as our rector."

"I'll second that," Steve says.

We vote then and stand up and applaud and stamp our feet.

Kati gathers up the agendas and starts crossing out "Priest-in-Charge" and writing in "Rector."

"Oh, shoot," Stefani says. "We don't have any champagne."

ON FRIDAY, I run into Mark, still shell-shocked, in the library.

"Can you tell me what was going on with you in that meeting?" I ask him.

"Yes," he says, sitting down. "At least, I think I can. I had it all worked out. I would wait until I got a reading at the workshop and then decide. I wanted to feel completely safe before I committed myself to Trinity and before the parish committed itself to me. But I realized in the meeting that it wasn't going to happen, that it wasn't"—he laughs—"going according to plan. And so when I walked back into the room, I felt very much as if I were jumping off a cliff. I was terrified. I mean, I was really terrified." He stops. Then he says quietly, "But you know, this is where I understand Pentecost. I felt God was there, in the jumping, in the falling. I don't want to minimize how terrified I was, and still am, but it was a holy terror."

On Sunday at the ten o'clock service, Elly stands up and says, "I have the joy today of introducing you to your new rector," and pandemonium breaks out. The entire congregation rises to its feet in a wave. They applaud, they stamp their feet, they whistle and shout. "This is entirely un-Anglican," Elly says laughing. Mark stands there in his green robes, the color for the Pentecost season—for living, greening, becoming—fighting back tears. I look over at Elaine and Steve. These two people got us into the boat, I think, and now we have pushed off from the shore.

. . .

IN THE NEXT WEEKS, a committee of the vestry prepares for the meeting in August while a larger, church-wide committee makes final plans for the Human Sexuality Workshop.

The Human Sexuality Committee, a broad group of parishioners, including several gay men (who are in varying degrees of openness at church), several heterosexual elderly women, and all varieties in between, has been meeting since February. The committee asked Jenny Ladefoged, a no-nonsense layperson who is the former chair of the Commission on Theology and Human Sexuality for the diocese, to lead the workshop. The committee has planned two sermons: one in August on Anglican ethics and a second one, in September, to be preached by Martha Siegel, on human sexuality. In August, a short forum entitled "Dialogue vs. Debate" will be led by Chris Boesch, who is studying mediation for her master's degree. No stone has gone unturned.

One of the plans for the workshop is for us to gather in "small groups" and tell stories about our lives in relation to sexuality. Everyone is nervous about this, of course. Michael Harris, of the vestry, says cheerfully, "As a conservative, I would like to say that I don't want to. I don't want to talk about sexuality or sex in public. I'm not coming."

As I think over my own life, two women come into my mind, women I had not thought about in years. Irene was a retired journalist who lived across the street from our family's house in Albuquerque. She'd moved to the dry and sunny Southwest in the forties because she had TB. She wore baggy pants and old sweaters and was gruff and smart. She taught me Chinese checkers and let me play with the toys she brought back from her many trips to India. (Each time I went to her house, I was invited to go to the small, special room where only the toys were kept and allowed to choose one.)

We had a regular routine. Irene and I would play three games of Chinese checkers; the winner of two was the champ.

Then her friend, Estella, would bring us tea and cookies on an elaborate tray with linen napkins. Estella was the archetypal grandmother: she was always dressed in freshly ironed cotton and had beautiful white hair that she wore braided and wound around her head. I knew as a child that she was a retired doctor, a fact significant to me, since I knew no other women who were doctors.

As we sipped our tea, they listened attentively to my ideas, and I had ideas about everything. To this independent and solitary child, they were the perfect companions. They never condescended to me, but treated me as if I and my ideas were as interesting to them as were those of an adult. I loved them. That there was anything "irregular" about them never entered my head.

Sometime in my adolescence, I figured it out. These were "lesbians," a word I had recently learned and viewed with terror. (Because I loved to hunker down in the dry winter irrigation ditches with my friend Elaine and read D. H. Lawrence, giggling together at the sex scenes, could I be one of *them*?) Although I was afraid of even a glimpse of homosexuality in myself, when I realized that Irene and Estella were lesbians I was neither disgusted nor frightened. Instead, I felt that a missing piece had fallen into place. Ah, of course, I remember thinking, that was why they felt the way they did. I reacted this way not because I was so wise or generous, but because of them: the rightness of their relationship, the sure knowledge that they loved each other, that they felt like and were a bonded couple. They were as married as my mother and father.

To have had these friends so early in my life forever colored my attitudes toward homosexuals. They were a part of my world growing up; they were loved and respected, and . . . what? Normal. As I held their memory, both of them dead now, I thought, This is a gift of this workshop.

AS THE PLANS for the workshop develop, it's clear that more than homosexuality needs to be addressed. "There are twenty years of questions," Mark says at one point. "There's divorce, living together, the sexual revolution. We haven't talked about any of this in church."

As he talks I wonder, Where has the Church been all these years? Where was the Church when I slept with my boyfriend in college? When I found the one doctor in town who would prescribe birth control pills to students? When, during an early and painful marriage, I wrestled with divorce? Where was the Church when I watched gay men in San Francisco in the seventies in a kind of sexual frenzy that had within it a hidden, and fragile, hope?

And I see, then, partly why I left the Church. It simply wasn't there for any of these events in my life, either to help me sort them out or to give them dignity. I could bring none of them with me when I prayed.

"When people at I. Magnin found out I was a priest," Mark said last year, "they often looked at me as if I were a relic. The Church was irrelevant to them."

This was partly how the Church became irrelevant. By standing on the sidelines or insisting on rigid standards while a whole generation dealt with sudden sexual liberation and confusion. And thus the Church lost a moral ground—a real moral ground, rather than what passed for one. "A corrupt version of Christianity says, unless you get . . . things absolutely right, you're going to hell," said Richard Holloway, the Bishop of Edinburgh, in an interview. "That is no way to help people be moral. You may scare them into conformity, but that is not morality."

I remember the woman at the newcomers' orientation last

year who said, "I want to bring my whole self to church." Me, too, I think, and then I see that through Mark we might open wide the door for everyone.

IN MID-AUGUST, just before the vestry is to meet at Judy's house, I sit down to read the morning paper and see a headline just below the fold. "Church Court to Try Bishop for Ordaining Gay," it reads. What was rumored in the spring has come to pass.

"In a move that is certain to escalate tension with Christian churches over gays in the clergy, an Episcopal bishop will face a trial in a rare church court for ordaining a gay man five years ago," the article reads. "[Bishop Walter] Righter ordained Barry Stopfel as deacon in September 1990, knowing that Stopfel was a non-celibate homosexual."

Ten conservative bishops, most of them from the South, have brought charges—called a presentment—against Bishop Righter, citing the 1979 resolution containing that last line, "We believe it is inappropriate for this Church to ordain a practicing homosexual. . . ." Seventy-six bishops have signed the presentment.

The presentment argues that the '79 resolution contains the force of doctrine; thus Righter is accused of "teaching false doctrine," or heresy. This is tenuous ground. The Episcopal Church is distinct in its lack, one might even say its abhorrence, of doctrine. Over the centuries, various Episcopal bodies have agreed to only a few sources of authority: Holy Scripture, the Nicene Creed, the Apostles' Creed, and the Book of Common Prayer. Belief in the Episcopal Church rests on Scripture, tradition, and reason, the so-called Anglican three-legged stool.

"There is not now, and there never has been, a distinctive

Anglican theology," writes W. Taylor Stevenson, in *The Study of Anglicanism*. "We have no Thomas or Luther, no Calvin or Zwingli. Nor is there any authority in Anglicanism which corresponds to the magisterium of the Roman Catholic Church."

The doctrine argument is both a smoke screen for the battle between liberals and conservatives in the Church over homosexuality and over sexuality in general (at least four of the bishops who brought the original presentment still will not ordain women as priests), and part of a larger disagreement. It reflects a struggle over the character of the Church: whether church tradition is to be interpreted broadly or narrowly, whether within the Church there is room for freedom and diversity—a diversity as old as that first Day of Pentecost—or whether there is less room, more order, and a final, unified authority. One of the authors of the presentment, Bishop James M. Stanton of Dallas, who happened to serve as a priest under Righter in Iowa when Righter was an active bishop, told the *New York Times*, "The question is, how do we bring order here? I believe in the principle of order and unity."

AS THE DAYS go by, George Barrett's file on the presentment grows fat with letters:

> To: The Most Reverend Edmond Browning,
> Presiding Bishop
> From: The Right Reverend William C. Wantland,
> Eau Claire, Wisconsin
> . . . Should this matter be brought to trial, it is our intention to file presentments against the next most recent offender, and so on, until we are current in bringing to trial all those who have knowingly violated the teaching of the church . . .

To: Certain Bishops of the Episcopal Church
From: The Right Reverend John S. Spong, D.D.,
Newark, New Jersey

. . . This church of ours is now to be thrown into a heresy trial over the ordination of gay people who have been screened and recommended by Commissions on Ministry and Standing Committees, and whose lives have been judged to be wholesome examples to the flock of Christ. . . . I, for one, am not willing simply to stand by idly and watch my church undergo this process . . . So I am proposing to join with those of you who so choose to seek to become a co-defendant with Walter Righter in his trial. . . . Whether or not you have actually ordained a gay or lesbian person to the priesthood is irrelevant to this stance. The issue is whether or not you believe you have the right to do so in conjunction with decision-making bodies of your diocese so long as there are not canonical prohibitions against this action . . .

To: The Right Reverend George Barrett
From: The Reverend James A. Hanisian, Episcopal
Church of the Redeemer, Cincinnati, Ohio

. . . But, I do not believe that the matter is about doctrine at all. The Church, as you rightly point out, is not going to get its doctrinal act together about this issue in the near future. We will, alas, argue instead of listen; look for half-way measures that do not solve anything; continue our liberal-conservative ideological debate until we make the average person in the pew wish she or he were a Methodist. On the issue of doctrine, I have believed for a long time there is nothing in a person's sexuality that would qualify or disqualify them for ordination. Behavior? That's another matter.

Nevertheless, the mind of the Church for the past six conventions, at least, has been not to ordain people sexually active outside the bond of Holy Matrimony. It is not our doctrine but our discipline that is at issue.

Those who seek to try Bishop Righter don't want to argue the matter of discipline because they, too, violate their ordination vows by refusing to accept or ordain women. Women's ordination is also not a matter of Church doctrine. It became our discipline in 1976— about ten years too late in my opinion.

Bishops in particular are sworn to uphold the discipline of the Church. . . . Some applaud Bishop Righter. Some seek to present him. On the issue, I think he's dead right. On the action, I believe he deserves to be convicted . . .

To: The House of Bishops
From: Saint George's Church, Maplewood, New Jersey
. . . In the many viewpoints expressed so far regarding the presentment against Bishop Righter, it seems that one very important aspect has been overlooked—namely the life and ministry of the people of Saint George's, under their Rector, the Reverend Barry Stopfel.

As the elected leaders of the Parish, we too struggle with the tension between doctrine and how we live out our faith. But one thing is clear; we are a body of people committed to upholding the Baptism vows that unite us as God's people. . . . To deny someone the right to follow their call and the right to prove their vocation to themselves and others, on the grounds of sexual orientation, we consider a sin. To deny people, who are so eager and anxious to hear the word of God as it applies to them, the fruits and richness of the ministries of these people, we consider a sin.

As the 21st century approaches, we need leaders in the church who are truly present in life's births and deaths, who embody the theology they uphold with their own life's experiences, who do not hide or shut themselves away behind canon law, who are not afraid to be honest with their peers, parishioners, friends and families. Our lives have been touched and changed by this individual and we thank God daily for giving us the opportunity of calling him to our parish. We thank Bishop Righter and Bishop Spong daily for their integrity, their belief and faith, and the great gift they gave us when they ordained Barry. . . .

JUDY BROWN'S HOUSE is a comfortable, Spanish-style place in Hope Ranch, an old subdivision near the ocean with a big artificial lake, palm trees, and a golf course. On a table as we come in is an array of coffee and iced tea. Kati brought homemade brownies.

Mark arrives in a blue shirt and khaki pants. Robert Hagler is right behind him, also dressed casually, in a polo shirt and khakis. Various vestry members straggle in.

We've read various documents including the Koinonia Statement, and we've been given a chronology of decisions by the church regarding gay men and lesbian women.

Robert calls the meeting to order. In his soft Tennessee drawl, he offers a prayer, and then begins:

"I'd like to start with some background. In the Church's conversation about sexuality, what needs to be present and hasn't been in official Church history or in the development of moral theology, is that we are dealing with human beings, with people. Sexuality doesn't exist in an abstract way. Conversations about sexuality have to take place within a community with the understanding that we are human beings. I must know that I am dealing with issues that are as present for the person sitting across from me as they are for me.

"It is difficult to talk about sex: your mother never asked you about your spirituality or your sexuality. I have seen this difficulty at our national conventions, in Phoenix and in Indianapolis. But we need to find the words, to create a language that people are comfortable using.

"In order to create a language, we must bring ourselves to the topic. We must learn to disclose ourselves to our communities in a way that helps create a way of speaking. The Incarnation is a theological framework for us in this conversation. In spite of the damage we've done in the realm of moral theology with sex and the body, we still have a framework in the Incarnation for talking about our sexual lives.

"With all that in mind, I want to tell you that I am a gay man myself. Without that disclosure, this conversation would not have the grounding it requires."

Robert pauses for a moment, and looks down at his hands. The room is silent.

"You know," he continues, "the old liberalism doesn't apply to what is going on now in the lives of gay people. The old liberalism said that it was all about privacy, that what you did in your bedroom was your business, but don't necessarily talk about it. I have heard many stories from people about coming out to their families, and most of them were accepted by their blood kin, but told, essentially, 'It's fine, I love you but I don't want to hear about it.' "

He looks around the room and smiles at Judy. "But you know, we must not only live with who we are, but we need to give voice to who we are. It's not about whether it's right or wrong to be gay, but can a gay person talk about being gay. It's such an important issue. Not wanting to hear about it is crippling to a person's human growth and development.

"And so getting a language for ourselves goes far beyond the issue of being gay. It's about how all of us can talk honestly about who we really are."

This is Robert's sermon, I think; he has given us his life.

After a pause, Steve says, "You know, Robert is trusting us with something not everyone knows. I think that's sort of where Mark is coming from. He's gotten to this point in his life where he knows he's got to start trusting people with very private information."

Another pause. Then Robert introduces Carol Bason.

"I'm a member of the church community, a wife, a mother of grown children, a psychotherapist, and a person who has deep love for the Church," she says. "I often find myself in a situation where I am asked to join church groups where there is a desire to talk at a deeper level, to know each other more clearly, to struggle with difficulties that are very hard. I would suppose"—she grins—"that's why I was invited to do this. I want to add that I love the Church and as a result I am really interested in inclusiveness and openness. If I can help that in a church community, that's what I like to do." She pauses, then says: "I see you have a list of questions to consider. Would you like to look at them?"

Various people reach for the paper with the questions:

4. How does a Vestry person make this ethical choice?
   a. Is gay lifestyle acceptable/unacceptable?
   b. Is this a social justice issue?
   c. How does a Vestry person decide?

"I've lived a sheltered life," Steve says. "Ten years ago, in a word association, if someone said 'homosexuality' to me, I would have said 'sin.' No one in my family is gay, as far as I know. When I lived in the Bay Area, I had gay friends but they were my 'gay friends.' And if someone had said 'a gay priest,' I would have said, 'Oh, no, no, no, What about our children?'

"But you know, when it feels right, you know it. It was a good fit with Mark from the beginning. I think we realized it before he did. And I thought, Okay, he's gay. This is the person for whom it is worth changing my opinion."

"That's really lovely, Steve," Carol says. Then she adds, "I have some questions I jotted down that I think we might look at. For instance, is there an embarrassment issue for you, if people identify Trinity with being a 'gay church'? What if the larger portion of parishioners are gay, and straight people are in the minority?

"My neighbor said to me the other day, 'Oh, you go to Trinity, that's the gay church,' " Steve says. "Not because he knows about Mark. He doesn't know about Mark. But because we did the AIDS Mass."

"Well, I don't want it to be a 'gay church,' if you mean that only gay people will come to church," Elaine says. "I want Trinity to be about a lot of people, families and seniors and gay people, too."

"It is a justice issue," Ed says. "We want Trinity to be open to gay men and lesbian women, and other people who may not have felt included at church. That's what 'inclusive' means. But it's not limited to gay people."

"You know, you have a choice, in our culture, to have a cultural Christianity or a committed Christianity," Robert says. "A cultural Christianity is a Christianity where you go to a nice church and you take your children to a nice church where you have a liturgy that pleases you without any depth of commitment. A committed Christianity challenges people to cross that bridge from a cultural inclination to a commitment in faith."

"Yes," says Elaine. "I think about that when I think about what to say to our children in Sunday school. We want our children to grow and change the world. We want them to grow in knowledge and in love of their neighbor. It's about a lot more than memorizing Bible verses."

"You know," Steve says, "I'm thinking about the difference between going at this in a political way and going at it in a faith community. I don't want to force anything down anyone's throat. I want to make room for a lot of different points of view."

"I agree," I say. And think, How does this work? Steve and I are at opposite ends of the political spectrum but we work together very well. It's something to do with shared belief: we believe, both of us, in the same Christ and in the love of God. It allows us to make room for "diversity," to make room for each other.

We break for snacks. I wander over to look at a collection of family photos on the top of a bureau. There's a younger picture of Judy, her tall husband, who died of a brain tumor twelve years ago, and their two children. They look intensely happy to be together.

"He had just been diagnosed," Judy says quietly to me. "I said, 'Let's get everyone together.' " She's quiet for a minute. Then she says, "I loved what Robert said. I have the feeling that he is a very spiritual person, quite a wonderful person, and so what he said, everything he said, and especially when he told us he was gay, it did a lot for my faith. It strengthened my feeling for Mark that homosexuality doesn't matter at all to one's faith and one's spiritual quality."

When we reconvene, Carol says she would like us to address a few more of the questions. "A few of the touchy ones. What about Mark's private life? Do you think that's the vestry business? For example, what happens if Mark should date?"

"You wish," Michael Harris says to Mark.

"Thank you for sharing that, Michael," Mark says.

"I would just like to treat Mark like any other priest," Elaine says. "I don't care if he dates."

Kati and Elly nod.

"What will we do about telling the parish?" Ed asks.

"I'm not sure we have to," replies Kati. "It's Mark's private life, after all."

"But if I were a parishioner and I found out about Mark by some other method," Ed says, "I would feel betrayed."

"But heterosexual priests don't have to stand up and say, 'I'm heterosexual,'" says Elaine.

"What about the Righter presentment?" asks Stefani. "Will that affect us?"

"I think it's going to take a while to sort that one out," Robert says. "I don't know that anyone knows."

"You know, I think we're going to have to just go through the sexuality workshop and take a pulse," Kati says. "And then figure out the next step. Mark's privacy is very important to me."

It's getting late. Robert has to get back to the monastery. Elly says she thinks we've discussed all we're going to discuss today. I look down at the sheaf of papers on the table in front of me. I had hoped to find an answer in this meeting as to what to do next, how to find a way for Mark to come out to the congregation, but we have no answers. Instead, we found out that all we can do is stay together until we find land.

As I walk him to his car, Robert says, "You know I feel like I just took the plunge. I feel like that conversation affirms my understanding of Catholicism—that is, that the church community is the realm of the Holy Spirit. I have this great sense of really having walked into the waters of our two-thousand-year-old tradition. The waters were the issues we were struggling with and it's refreshing and revitalizing to be in those waters. I felt that offering that part of myself for the fuller community was like offering it for the regenerating waters of baptism. It was like having that part of me," he says, getting into his Honda Accord, "baptized."

D RIVING HOME ON the freeway one evening the following week, I find myself thanking God, a small set of prayers. Thank God for the witness of Robert Hagler. For the young man I just met with in Ventura, who is large and edgy, wears an earring, and is always cheerful: "For Peter," I say almost aloud. For the young woman editor I work with who has a great laugh, works hard, and is trying to raise a baby daughter by herself: "For Kim," I say. For the ocean that I am passing, for the sunny day in an unusually foggy summer, for the smell of Vincent's skin this morning when I kissed him good-bye. Soon I'm on a roll, there are so many things to be thankful for, in just one day.

In a rabbinic story, it is suggested that one carry blessings in two pockets, one on each side. The idea is that they must balance each other. My friend, Laurie Gross, a Jewish artist, carries these "blessings" in her two pockets: on the right, "For me the world was created," and on the left, "I am dust and ashes."

O N SATURDAY MORNING in late August the days seem to suddenly grow shorter. The angle of light lowers. I place my regular weekly call to Kit. He says he's feeling pretty good, although he has had to "use the catheter" a lot in the field.

"What does your doctor say about that?" I ask.

"He says he thinks it might be scar tissue," Kit replies. "They might have to ream me out."

"Ouch. When do you have another CAT scan?"

"I'm scheduled for one in September."

We graduate out of this talk to other matters. To Rob, his second son, who is working at the Very Large Array, a series of antennas near Socorro. I like everything about the VLA, starting with its name. (Or the Very Huge Array, I think to myself. Or the Very, Very Big Array.) Driving near Socorro with Kit, Rande, and Vincent one evening, a light snow rushing across the two-lane road, we came around a corner and there they were: white saucers like giant morning glories, rising up from the perfectly flat Plains of San Augustin. A project of the National Science Foundation, the antennas receive radio waves from space and process them with the help of very large computers. Recently, the VLA observed a body in orbit which at first appeared to be a sun moving around another sun. As they processed the data, however, they found that the size of one of the suns would have to be three to five times more massive than our own sun. In addition, no light was emitted from this larger object. The theory that finally fit this data was that the larger body was a black hole. "The only thing in the universe that speaks loudly while not saying anything," as Rob said to me.

"Rob's running up too many debts," Kit says.

"I did that in my twenties."

"Well, I didn't."

"You sound like a father."

"I am a father."

"Yeah, well, you weren't exactly Mr. Middle Class when you were in your twenties."

"Yeah, well, that's true. He's a very good guy. He's helping me with the water system." Then, switching gears, he says. "And how are you? Are you all right? You sound tired."

"I'm working too hard."

"Listen, baby sister, don't work too hard. Get some rest. Can you and Vincent go to Big Sur? Go up to Big Sur and give my regards to the redwoods."

"I'll try."

"You try. You are my only sister and I love you very much."

And then I am crying. "You are my only brother," I say. "And I love you very much."

AT THE THURSDAY evening Eucharist, Martha consecrates the elements using a prayer by Janet Morley: "Come now, disturbing Spirit of our God, breathe on these bodily things and make us one body in Christ. Open our graves, unbind our eyes and name us here; touch and heal all that has been buried in us that we need not cling to our pain but may go forth with power to release resurrection in the world."

At the base community that night, there is an empty chair at the end of the table, where Lois regularly used to sit.

We end up talking about the Holy Spirit as the one who speaks to the imagination. Metaphor—the language of the imagination—breaks open the old container.

"Imagination is our chief way of loving in ourselves and in others what is useless," writes James Carroll in *A Terrible Beauty*. "It is the source and the basis of the community we seek with each other. And what is more, imagination is what makes it possible for us to be religious people."

"The labyrinth speaks to the imagination," Ann Jaqua says. "Sometimes I think it speaks two languages, the language of the street and the language of the soul."

"The Holy Spirit may be the gift of imagination, may be the spark of fire that fills us with desire for the future," says Dodie. "Our work is to imagine the unimaginable."

"Maybe sin, among other things," says Mark Benson, "is the failure to imagine."

I say that I've been thinking of the labyrinth in the context of "the communion of saints," or Dorothy Day's "communion of workers." I'm thinking of the labyrinth as a gift from the artists who conceived and made it, a gift from the Middle Ages. I see them handing us this gift through the barrier of time, and in that giving, finding a passage through both time and death. They are alive in the gift of the labyrinth: we make one, and they live again.

At compline a line from an old prayer passes through my thoughts: "in which we live and move and have our being."

At the end of August, I receive a postcard from Anne Howard, who is on vacation: "Have a thought about Pentecost: it's about being not yet, not finished, on the way, the only season like that . . . more later on this."

Ordinary Time

IN THE BOOK OF EXODUS are directions for making an altar: it's to be square, built of acacia—a light, fast-growing, desert tree—and overlaid with gold. Inside it must be "hollow"; no idol should reside there: inside is both presence and absence. Four rings are to be fastened to its four corners. Through the rings, the Hebrew people are to put two poles, hoist the altar on their shoulders, and carry it with them wherever they go. Nomads, traveling with their herds, they created a theology of journey. "Wherever you go, I will go," says Ruth to Naomi. Not only will God be found in the sacred places marked by mounds of stones and fixed altars, but also in the journey to them.

The road to the sacred is paved with the ordinary. In the spring of 1990, just after the Berlin Wall came down, I was on a train between Prague and Vienna. With me in the "first-class" compartment (dirty pink upholstery and torn lace doilies, deeply imbedded smell of pork grease) were two Germans, a woman and a man. She was dressed in a black sweater and long wool skirt; her chestnut hair fell down her back. He looked like an academic of a different era, right down to his tight tweed jacket. We were all about the same age, born after the war.

After briefly greeting each other, each of us was quietly reading. Her head was bent over a sheaf of papers, and he read a thick book. After an hour or so, she produced a bar of chocolate from her pocket; he offered a piece of cheese. I pulled out what was left of an apple strudel. She said she was traveling from Berlin to Vienna, for a conference on how to write a screenplay. I was writing an article about families in Prague. And then he said, looking at her, "I am coming from the GDR [the German Democratic Republic, East Germany] to a meeting of psychoanalysts in Vienna. It is my first trip to the West." They looked at each other, gravely, without smiling, and fell to talking, in English at first, out of politeness to me, but finally in German. The compartment grew soft and dark. On their faces was revealed, as pain often surfaces just as it is assuaged, the private ache of almost thirty years of separation. The train rolled on. They leaned forward more and more as they talked; his hands held tight to his knees. They were, as John Berger writes in his book of the same title, "keeping a rendezvous." It was only an hour in my life and in the life of the universe, but they were giving, as Berger writes, "the whole of themselves to the moment being lived, when Being and Becoming are the same thing." I saw in them the material out of which hope is made, a glimpse of the kingdom. As we came into Vienna, they leaned back.

In answer to a question regarding the afterlife, Henry David Thoreau is said to have replied, "One world at a time." It is here, all around us, the kingdom we seek, in ordinary things and in time, in what we allow into us.

On the Hanging Gardens trail above Jenny Lake in Wyoming, Vincent's aunt, Malinda, named the flowers on the side of the trail: monkshood and pearly everlastings. Her daughter, Claire, who was then eleven, said she'd found an aspen grove she named Claire's Bliss. Yesterday, hunched in my rose garden working on a drip system with my gray tabby cat, both of us drowsy in the September sun, I looked up and saw a green blade of grass, and beyond it the translucent pink paper of a late hollyhock. I was absorbed into them, was, as my friend Joanne says, "both accepted and enchanted."

For a Eucharist prayer Roy Parker sings a version of e. e. cummings: "We thank you God for this amazing day / For leaping greenly spirits of trees / And a blue true dream of sky / And for everything which is natural / Which is infinite, which is Yes."

"The wisdom of the tree," Thomas Jayawardene, a priest from Sri Lanka, preaches this morning. "The secrecy of its bark, the silence of its leaves."

As he preaches I look around at the people in the chairs. Elizabeth Corrigan in a bright blue suit sits ahead of me. Next to her is her second son, Patrick, a tall gray-haired man in a blazer and khaki pants. He turns and smiles, and Dan is there for a second and then he is gone. Ahead of him, Elizabeth Reifel's cloudy hair floats above her linen jacket. Next to me is a dark-haired woman, raised in a household of atheists, who has just joined Trinity, having never been to church in her life. (She calls herself our "student rep.") She blows a kiss to her daughter, sitting in the front row with her Sunday school class. The girl reaches up, "catches" it with her right hand, places it against her cheek.

Hidden in each of us are our histories—depression, divorce, bulimia, layoffs, adultery, abuse—the wreckage of late-twentieth-century lives, our debris. And with it the healed family, the happy second marriage, a found vocation, the long-awaited birth. We are living in the intimacy of community, carrying the altar of our lives. Isabelle is pregnant at last, Nathan is a year old, Mark is our rector. Where there was an empty church, now it is full.

In most of the other church seasons, we trace the life of Jesus—from expected arrival to resurrection, Advent to Eastertide. But in Ordinary Time we are in our own lives, living out the gift of the Holy Spirit at Pentecost, "living out the reverberation from that beat of a butterfly wing," as Mark put it last week, "on its way to the ends of the universe."*

One of Mark's classmates from The General Theological Seminary, Carr Holland, the rector of a church in New Jersey, came to visit and preach at Trinity in the last weeks of August. A slim, dark-haired man, he talked openly in his sermon about his recent divorce, his love for his daughter, and his desire that he and his former wife make peace with each other. He said, "When we bring our real needs to prayer, when we pray that our real needs be met, our real need for love, our hunger for justice, our yearning for freedom, then we are saying, 'Let us see, in our real needs met, the foreshadowing of your reign.'

"Often we are afraid to ask for what we want or desire," he went on, "but the way of discernment is to lay out our desire and then come back to it with openness, seeking the wisdom of examination. Is this a need? Is there a deeper need? Is your reign foreshadowed here?"

Foreshadowing, the smallest progress, a glimpse of light.

One Sunday evening, I can't figure out what's wrong with me. I stomp around the house, ready to attack Vincent, anything to get rid of this suffering. But instead I hold my breath and just say it: "I'm falling apart. I think I need to do that. But I'm afraid you'll disappear if I do."

"I'm not going anywhere," he replies. "I'll be here, cooking dinner. You go ahead."

"Let me help you," I say to him the next week.

"No," he replies. "This bad time belongs to me."

"Oh," I say, and feel, first, anger and rejection, but then a clarity, a separation, and relief.

---

*The last months of the Christian year are a continuation of the Pentecost season in the Episcopal Church, but in the Roman Catholic Church, the season after Pentecost is called Ordinary Time. Although I'm departing from my own denomination's calendar with this chapter title, I like the idea of an "ordinary" season.

In the midst of our needs, we are waylaid by compassion. Jesus, walking through the crowds, suddenly finds a Greek woman at his feet, begging him to heal her daughter. His immediate answer is, basically, I've come for my own people, not you. She replies, "Even the dogs are given crumbs off the table."

He stops. You can picture the scene. The young rabbi, sure of his call, is suddenly offered a new reality. It comes up from the grass, from the rabble at his feet.

"Go," he says softly. "Your daughter is healed."

At the Kitchen in the serving line, one of the volunteers asks me if we can start serving seconds.

"Not yet," I say, irritated. "It's not twenty after."

"We've got a lot of soup," she says.

At the periphery of my vision, I see a woman standing near the table, clasping her soup bowl to her dirty shirt.

"Go ahead," I say to the volunteer.

"We have seconds," the volunteer says happily.

"Seconds," the woman says, coming forward. "That's a miracle."

ON MY BIRTHDAY, Anne Howard hands me a white square box. Inside in tissue paper is a perfectly round white stone with flecks of the palest green. "From Iona," she says. "One of St. Columba's 'marbles.' "

Another stone arrives in the mail from Kit and Rande, a flat one painted with Kokopelli, a Hopi trickster carrying a flute. "Rande is making these," Kit says in his card. "He's for good fortune all around. Hope you are doing o.k. Please call me if there is *anything* I can do for you. I love you."

Chris Boesch sends me a flat tan stone smooth as powder, to carry in your pocket, she says, whenever you're worried. I heap the stones on my desk, my own altar.

Ben Hitz comes over for tea. In his hands are a small box and an envelope. He opens the envelope first and takes out a picture of Lois in the Anza-Borrego desert. She's leaning on a rock, wearing a white long-sleeved T-shirt and shorts, low hiking boots. In her breast pocket are a flat notebook and two pencils ("For flower and plant sightings," Ben says). She has a wry smile on her face, as if to say, Well, here I am, now what?

As he opens the box, Ben says, "For her birthday and for various anniversaries, I gave Lois jewelry. I had it made often by a guy we both liked in Palos Verdes. I would like you to have one of these. I brought a selection." Out of the box he takes two silver bracelets, one with a clear stone that has brownish-gold streaks in it, like russet, like pieces of sequoia bark.

"Rutiliated quartz," Ben says.

The other is larger, with a black stone. I try on the smaller one first, and like it immediately. Then I remember it on Lois's wrist, one night at the base community.

"You keep that," Ben says.

AT THE BASE COMMUNITY, the Gospel is Luke 15:1–10.

"Now all the tax collectors and sinners were coming near to listen to him. And the Pharisees and the scribes were grumbling and saying, 'This fellow welcomes sinners and eats with them.' So he told this parable: Which one of you, having a hundred sheep and losing one of them, does not leave the ninety-nine in the wilderness and go after the one that is lost until he finds it? When he has found it, he lays it on his shoulders and rejoices. And when he comes home, he calls together his friends and neighbors, saying to them, 'Rejoice with me, for I have found my sheep that was lost.' Just so, I tell you, there will be more joy in heaven over one sinner who repents than over ninety-nine righteous persons who need no repentance.' "

In one translation, the last line is "There will be joy in heaven over one person who has a change of heart."

"There's a refrain in the Gospels, of lost and found," Ann Jaqua says. "Of being lost, being found."

"I think of my sister as the lost one," someone says. "She's the one in the family who has always needed the most finding."

"It seems that we have to be lost to be found," Dodie says. "We have to be the Prodigal Son in order to return. It is so much about this kind of journey."

"I think we take turns being the lost one," Ann replies.

"It makes me wonder what Jesus' life in his twenties was like," Dodie says. "If he got to know these lowlifes and saw the good in them, what was he doing?"

We check in. Elizabeth Reifel says she has a friend whose daughter had a sudden heart attack on the dance floor and is in a coma. She has been trying to pray for her, for the family, but has found a block between her and the prayer, or between her and God. Finally, today, she says, "I gave it over."

Katrina says Martha Siegel has given her a tape to listen to called *Warming the Stone Child.*

"It's about finding the mother inside you," she says firmly. Then she adds that a young man moved into their house, started drinking, and was asked to leave. He threatened Katrina and her housemates. The police arrested him and put him in jail. The district attorney asked their advice as to what to do with him.

"We told him we don't want to punish him," she says. "We want to help him, but we don't know exactly how. It seemed to us that he might need the containment of jail for a few days, but then what? We told the D.A. he should be in a program that would first help him stop drinking and then address the problems he had that led to the drinking. And," she says with a small smile, "the D.A. did exactly what we told him."

"My husband's back at work," Nancee says, "the kids are in school. I flit around the house. I have stacks of things to do and I'm wondering, now that I'm done with graduate school, what will I do?"

Ann says she's noticed a small crop of weedlike plants in her graveled yard. She waited to see if they were actually weeds, before she pulled them. When the second leaves grew, they were soft. "They turned out to be lamb's ears," she says. "I have this whole crop of lamb's ears. And I realized, once again, that this is the reason I'm trying to slow down and not do too much. It is to notice that I have lamb's ears growing wild in my garden."

Mark Benson says he had a dream about Philip, that Phil was in his rose garden, "among the David Austins. When I'm in the rose garden, I feel as if I am in another world. You know the biblical line about things passing, and things that endure? Phil is where things endure."

I talk about something that happened over the weekend. I was lying on the window seat in the evening, looking up at the pine tree outside. I'd had cataract surgery a few days before, and my surgeon didn't know why my eyesight hadn't improved. I was to wait a week. I was as scared as I have been in my life, in a new kind of terror, the terror that I would not heal, that my body, so dependable, would not or could not restore itself. I felt lonely. Other people my age, my friends, even Vincent, could not know what this was like, and therefore I could not find solace. Then I thought of Lois. At some point in her life, Lois had received the news that she had ovarian cancer. She had somehow gone on living after that. I could not imagine how she had done it; how she had managed to come to the base community, to describe hunting mushrooms in the hills or the flowering of the desert. How had she done it? Just then, I felt her presence. I felt, particularly, the skin of her hands. They felt dry and sunny, as if she were holding a piece of the sun. I felt her presence and heard her voice inside my head: the voice sounded exactly like Lois, and she said something like "Things will improve." It was as matter-of-fact as what she had said when Kit was first diagnosed, "This is the worst time." Lois had no platitudes; her solace came directly from experience.

The overall feeling of this whatever-it-was was of detached kindness, without emotion, clarity without sentiment, the purity and refreshment of a sun-dried sheet. Several days later I read in C. S. Lewis's *A Grief Observed* his account of being visited by Joy, his dead wife: "No sense of joy or sorrow. No love even, in our ordinary sense. No un-love. I had never in any mood imagined the dead could be so—well, so business-like. Yet there was an extreme and cheerful intimacy. An intimacy that had not passed through the senses or the emotions at all."

I lay there, feeling her hands and hearing her voice, and I was full of gratitude. Then I decided to test whether this was a real "visitation" by asking her, in my mind, to tell me what it was like "on the other side." I asked and she evaporated. I could not call her back. I tried. I tried by remembering her, by conjuring, literally, her face and her hair, but it was completely different from the way it had been just minutes before. Before, it was Lois. Now, it was my mind, my memory, my imagination. I saw the distinction very clearly: the ghost part of a ghostly encounter may be the faded memory, the overworked imagination. This Lois had hardly been a ghost; she was a vivid felt presence, but removed. One step.

Elizabeth Reifel says, "That's comforting."

THE FIRST OF the Human Sexuality Workshops comes up in late September. We have freighted this event with so much that when it arrives, we are all running around like the proverbial chickens.

"Who will introduce Jenny?" my anxious notes read. "Registration person? Card tables? Name tags? Tea? Set of remote microphones. Easel. Pens. Tape. Mark has map. Someone to take notes? Locations for small group discussions. Clarify small group topics."

Jenny arrives from Los Angeles twenty minutes before the workshop is to begin, dressed in a dark long dress that accentuates her height.

Fifty people have signed up. As they arrive, my cursory glance sees mostly the liberals of the parish. Then Linda arrives, a thin woman who is conservative, a pensive frown on her face.

Jenny opens the workshop by asking each one of us to say where we were born.

"Oakland, California."

"Albuquerque, New Mexico."

"Cowpens, South Carolina," says Terry Roof, a teacher who also does prison ministry.

Another southern voice pipes up from behind me, "Cowpens! I know where that is."

"You do?" Terry replies, turning around.

"It's hard to talk about sex," Jenny opens. "And nearly impossible to talk about sex in church. But the national church has asked us to do so because at the Episcopal General Convention in Phoenix in 1991 the bishops found themselves unable to agree on various position papers put forth regarding human sexuality. So the national church decided that they would ask every parish to hold discussions on the issue and report back.

"And how are we, as Christians, to address this fundamental human subject? We can ignore it and hope it will go away. Or we can try to find ways to talk, and think, without invading each other's privacy. I do not think it's easy, but I've done it with other parishes and you would be amazed at what has come up. One church in which I taught a workshop, about twenty-five people came and there were older women who talked about what they had done as teenagers. Their kids just sat there with their mouths open. It was a superb dialogue between two generations.

"We're not going to teach anything; there is not going to be any laying down of the ethics of the Church or what the Church teaches. It's going to be a dialogue, I hope.

"Anything said in the room should stay in the room. But we can't guarantee confidentiality, we can only beg for it. I always say at a workshop: If you want to come out or if you want to say you murdered your wife in another life, now is not the time unless you want everyone to know.

"And also, as you know, a bishop of the Episcopal Church has been 'presented' this summer for ordaining an openly gay man to the priesthood," Jenny continues. "We may want to talk about that."

She scans the room. Behind her open and casual face, I can see the radar.

After some initial discussion, she says, "I wonder if you'd like to do an exercise in imaging?" Uncertain, we agree.

"First, I want to give you a little background. Mary Magdalene is often thought of as a prostitute, although there is not a shred of evidence in the Bible to that effect. It may be that she is confused with the woman caught in adultery. Magdalene did have some kind of mental illness or a psychotic episode. She is referred to as 'possessed by demons.' Jesus healed her. And afterward she traveled with him and his friends. She was the first to see the risen Christ. She was therefore a disciple, but this is rarely if ever mentioned in the Church. Instead, she has this shadow reputation, a loose woman, a prostitute.

"Then there is the woman caught in adultery. We wonder, after that terrible scene in the square, when Jesus prevented the crowd from stoning her to death, what happened to her?

"And so I want you to close your eyes and put yourself in this scene," Jenny says. "A large house, a party going on inside. Men and women laughing and talking, you can hear their voices drifting outside through the open windows. You are sitting outside, on a bench, near the front steps. You have a shawl around you. You are Mary Magdalene. You have not been invited in.

"A man and a woman arrive at the party and go up the steps. They see you, and they look away."

I sit in the chair with my eyes closed, feeling slightly silly. Then, I "feel" the cold of the stone bench. I look up and "see" a man and a woman coming up the steps.

"They are dressed in fancy clothes, a dinner jacket on the man, a silk dress on the woman. The woman whispers something to the man, and then they both look at you, briefly, then laugh and look away."

I see them. I see the whisper, her mouth against his ear, and the laugh. A series of memories well up in me and with them, shame.

At fifteen, in love for the first time, I burned with erotic passion. He was seventeen, with brown arms and thick blond curls. Standing in the kitchen of a friend's house where I worked as the summer baby-sitter, he said, "I want to kiss you." We kissed in the corners of the swimming pool. We nestled together in his family's house in Santa Fe while he read to his younger brother, imitating a family. One night, we went for a drive near his family's summer house in northern New Mexico in his blue Hudson with the huge backseat. I was in a pale blue drop-waisted summer dress. We necked and necked until he opened his pants and came against my thigh; the semen soaked into my dress. I was a girl and not a girl, my virginal blue dress stained with semen. Only two years before, I had not yet menstruated. When we returned to his family's house, his older sister and his parents were playing poker in the kitchen. They seemed far away. I was dizzy with potency.

Then we were caught. Paul's hand in my shirt in our family's living room. Humiliated, my privacy invaded, afraid of what I was doing, I confessed just how far we had gone in the past and agreed to the order—even though I knew it was impossible that I was pregnant—that I rush to a pharmacy and buy a douche. The juicy desire in me became hidden and shameful. Bad girls and good girls, girls who go all the way, women who are easy. As I sit here, stunned by the amount of pain rising up in me, I think, if it is like this for me, what is it like for them?

"The man and the woman go inside," Jenny says. "You are alone, on the bench. Then you see someone coming toward you, another woman. You prepare yourself for another humiliation, but she comes over to you and sits down. She is the woman caught in adultery. She says to you, 'Mary.' "

At the name, I begin to cry.

" 'Mary,' she says. " 'I've come to sit with you because for so long you've been mistaken for me. It was I who sinned, not you. Although I do wonder about the nature of my sin and why the man with whom I was caught was never punished.' "

Then Jenny is silent. The room is still. I can hear behind me another woman crying.

"Slowly, now, I'd like you to begin to leave this scene," Jenny says. "Slowly, allow yourself to come back to this room. You may wait for a bit before you open your eyes."

Terry Roof hands me a Kleenex.

"Does anyone want to talk about what this experience was like for them?"

Behind me, Jennifer Borrmann raises her hand.

"I am that woman, that was me," she says, wiping her eyes. "I've been sexual all my life, and I have paid for it. I've felt like a slut."

"Where do you see God fitting in with your sexuality?" Jenny asks.

"Well, when I have an orgasm I say 'O God, O God,' " Jennifer says. Everyone laughs, a nervous bark.

"But you know, I wonder if this is more serious, actually," Jennifer says. "I mean I wonder if union with God is actually like, well, like an orgasm."

"Maybe that's the ultimate of being in touch with God," Terry Roof says. "Maybe we really will feel as good."

A number of women, including one in her seventies, nod and grin little excited smiles.

I think of Mechthild of Magdeburg, a thirteenth-century German mystic who left these lines: "My limbs shrivel, cramp torture every vein / My heart dissolve in loving you / My soul burn as the roar of a hungry lion / How shall it be with me then? / Where wilt Thou be then? Beloved, tell me!"

Mark Asman raises his hand. "I couldn't imagine being a woman," he says. "I mean, I really tried, and I could not do it. Then I thought, What is it like for women to hear on Sunday morning, 'Father, Son and Holy Spirit?' Or 'Our Father who art in Heaven'? I mean, if it's so hard for me to imagine myself as a woman, maybe it's just as hard for women to put themselves into that language."

A ripple of relief moves through the women in the room. This is turning out differently than I thought.

For the small-group discussions in the afternoon, we can choose from several questions. Among them: "With the many changes in our society, how do we define 'family'?" "If your son or daughter told you he or she was a homosexual, how would you want him or her treated by the church?" "What if your mother decided to live with a man without marrying him?"

Our group, six people, seated in the parish hall on our new white plastic chairs, includes Martha Smith, a widow, the

woman who was reluctant to walk the labyrinth but brave
enough to give it a try. Martha is wearing a beautiful red-and-
gold shawl around her shoulders. This afternoon she says she
thinks homosexuals are fine, really, she has no argument with
them, "Just as long as they don't get married."

When I ask her why not, she replies thoughtfully, "It was
ingrained in me from childhood. God created man and woman
and said, 'Go forth and multiply.' "

When we return to the larger group, Jenny asks us to
report, if we want to, on what was said.

Mandy McCoy, a computer software designer relatively
new to Trinity, raises her hand. "The question we chose was
'What is a family?' " she says. "We said that there were many
different ways that people could be a family. For example, if
two men lived together and they were partners—"

Linda interrupts. "No, we said they would be roommates,
not a family."

Mandy puts her hand on her hip. "Well, obviously we
didn't agree on this as a group."

At the end of the day, we gather for a Eucharist, using a
prayer from Janet Morley:

> *God our lover*
> *in whose arms we are held,*
> *and by whose passion we are known:*
> *require of us also that love*
> *which is filled with longing,*
> *delights in the truth,*
> *and costs not less than everything,*
> *through Jesus Christ, Amen.*

At the next workshop, Jenny asks for volunteers for a role
play. "I would like two women, who are going to role-play lesbians, and another woman, who will role-play an Episcopal

priest. The idea is that these two women want to be married in the church and the priest has to figure out what to do."

Terry Roof and Terry Walker, a former Roman Catholic nun who is now a business consultant, raise their hands. Then Dodie raises hers.

"Okay," Jenny says. "You two"—pointing to the two Terrys—"are the couple. And you, Dodie, are the priest."

The two Terrys sit down in front of Dodie.

"Hi," Terry Walker says. "We're in love and we want to get married."

"Yes," says Terry Roof. "We've been coming here to church for years now and we want our love for each other confirmed, affirmed, by the Church."

Dodie presses her hands to her temples.

"I don't think I have the right to do that at this time. I mean, I guess I'll have to think about it," she says.

"Can't you do it on your own?" Terry Walker asks.

"I don't know," Dodie says. "I don't think I can. I mean, I think I'll have to talk to the vestry. I might be able to perform a private ceremony in my office."

"We don't want to do that," Terry Walker says. "We want to stand up in front of the church, like everyone else."

"I wonder if being approved by the hierarchy is more important to you than the two of us," Terry Roof says.

Dodie shakes her head. "No, it isn't like that. I just can't, at this time . . ."

The three of them stand up.

"I have hope for the future," Dodie says.

"The future for us is now," Terry Roof replies.

The three women return to their seats.

"Well, what do you think?" Jenny asks the group,

Terry Roof says, "I kept remembering the civil rights movement in the South. People kept saying, 'You're going too fast.' I remembered how the Church failed us, failed me, by standing on the sidelines most of the time. I left the Church during civil rights. All of that went through my head during that role-play and I said to myself, This is the very same thing."

"The Bible is very clear on homosexuality," Linda says. "It says it's an abomination."

"You know, people are born the way they are," says Susan Stewart Potter, a playwright. "Why would you want to say anything about a person's inclinations or inability to be just like you? Isn't God the judge of this?"

"It's the act, not the people," Linda says.

"But it becomes the people, if you condemn the act," Susan replies.

"I have the verses from the Bible," Linda replies. "At home, I mean. I can show them to you."

"Well, show them to me tomorrow," Susan says.

"I will," Linda says. "I will."

At the end of the day, Jenny says, "You know, this is a room full of liberals. I have done workshops in a room full of conservatives. Have mercy on those who disagree with you."

Mark asks everyone to stick around for a few minutes and give us their thoughts on what was important to them about the workshops and where we might go from here. Terry pulls a flip chart into the room and writes with a blue Magic Marker.

"Teenagers and sexuality," says one person.

"Sexual abuse and misconduct," says another.

"Just relationships, getting by."

"The blessing of same-sex unions," says Dodie.

"That it?" asks Mark. "Well, let's do something that is un-Episcopalian. Let's stand in a circle for prayer and hold hands."

"Our Father," he begins, hesitates, then continues, "who art in Heaven."

"Hallowed be thy name."

When we have finished, Terry Roof rolls up the sheets

from the flip chart, puts a rubber band around them, and carries it out the door.

In a couple of weeks, she offers to host a follow-up meeting at her comfortable house near the church. Over pizza and salad, a group of thirty people, most of whom attended the workshops, chat and introduce themselves.

"I grew up in Utah," says a middle-aged man newly arrived from Baltimore. "When I came out, I became an oxy-Mormon."

Mandy McCoy is there, with her boyfriend, Tom Painter, who is working on his Ph.D. at the university. Mandy says her family is conservative, from the South, and that she grew up thinking homosexuality was a sin, but changed her mind when she left home.

"It means a lot to me that we reflect on this as a church community," she says in her soft drawl.

We look at the ideas on the flip-chart sheets and come up with three priorities: teenagers, same-sex blessings, the daily work of relationships.

"Which one should we work on first? Shall we vote?" Terry asks.

"I think the important thing to remember before you vote," Mark says nervously, "is that this group may end up as an advisory committee to the vestry. But advisory, remember."

George Barrett clears his throat. "Yes, remember: we are not a congregational church. That is, we don't vote as a body on things. This kind of thing is up to the rector. He decides. He can take or ask for advice, but it's his decision and his decision alone."

We vote. "And the winner is . . ." Terry says, "the blessing of same-sex unions." She smiles. "I can live with that. Let's meet in a month, same time, same place."

. . .

WHEN WE WALK into the library for the base community, a small Latino man with a ring of curls is sitting in a chair at the head of the table. He's wearing white sweatpants under a pair of white Bermuda shorts and a thin shirt. He introduces himself as Javier. When we check in, Javier keeps his head mostly in his hands. When it's his turn to speak, he says he's been depressed lately and is not clear what he should do in his life.

The Gospel is the story about the rich man and the beggar. In the story, the beggar lies at the gates of the rich man's house, but the rich man ignores him, gives him nothing, and so he dies. Later, the rich man himself dies. He goes directly to Hell. There he sees, far off, the beggar cradled in Abraham's arms in Heaven. A great gulf separates them; the rich man cannot cross it.

"You know, this story may not be about 'eternal damnation,' " Ann Jaqua says. "But instead it may be a description of reality. If one goes through life without seeing the beggar lying at the gate, if that person is invisible to you, you may get to the point where you see less and less and then not at all. Finally, you can't see God. The chasm becomes too wide. God becomes invisible."

Robin looks up. "This reminds me of when I was working as a temporary—remember? Last year? In that company that makes sandals. They were showing me around the office. And we came to a door. They passed by it. I said, 'What's in there?'

" 'Nothing,' they replied. Then the door opened; someone walked through. Inside were all these Hispanic people working at machines. It was very crowded and hot. And I had the weirdest sensation. I wanted to go inside. I wanted to go and be with them rather than outside, with the other office workers."

I'm thinking about that when Javier speaks up.

"I spent today walking, trying to find a place to take a nap, in shoes too big for me that someone gave me. The shoes hurt my feet. Night before last I slept outside without a blanket. It was too cold to sleep, so I spent most of the night walking. Toward morning I came across a number of men who were sleeping in sleeping bags and the heat they gave off was enough to warm me. I stood next to them, trying to absorb the heat, and almost fell asleep standing up. When one of them woke up at dawn, he gave me a piece of blanket and I sat down and put it over my shoulders and slept for about an hour."

When he finishes talking, a silence falls on us like a heavy curtain. I can't speak. I finally realize that in the face of that pain, silence is the only response that gives it dignity. We are not yet, it seems, in a place where what we say can comfort. We are not like the women in Nicaragua who could comfort because of their intimate knowledge of poverty.

Instead, we live in a machine that manufacturers consumers. Things blind us, crowd our vision. When the base community read the Gospel about the man who sold his field for "a pearl of great price," I thought, What would I sell for the kingdom? The 850 Volvo? The Maytag?

In our midst is a man without a blanket and shoes too large for his feet. We have organized our lives so that he is hidden from us. He lives, like God, in invisibility. But when we do see him, I think tonight, we keep a rendezvous. In the seeing is a glimpse, a foretaste of the kingdom: it will be a place where everyone is seen, including us. Here we are together, in Ordinary Time, learning how to see.

KIT CALLS ON Sunday morning, his voice light and cheerful.

"CAT scan is clean," he says.

"Yes!" I yell.

"They did it on Tuesday and Dr. Ortolano called me yesterday afternoon. They can't see a thing. It looks real good."

"Thank God," I say.

"Yes," Kit replies. "I do thank Him. In other news, it's getting colder at night. The apricot tree still has its leaves. Here Boy got into a fight yesterday and cut up his nose. I'm still getting tired during the day, having trouble keeping up with the guys, so my boss has me doing more paperwork at home."

"What's the paperwork like?"

"Figuring all kinds of geometry, angles. I'm using math I haven't used since college. It's pretty interesting, actually, but it takes a while to get my focus. Oh, the horse at the end of the street is pregnant. She'll have her colt in the spring. But I'm going on and on, what's up with you?"

Nothing much, I say, working, going to church.

"So, you're coming right after Christmas."

"So, we're coming right after Christmas."

"How are your eyes?"

"Improved," I reply and then laugh.

AT THE VESTRY MEETING, we talk first about the workshop.

"What did people think?" Mark asks.

"I was there only a short time," Elly says. "But I think it was fine. I just didn't get a sense that anyone is very upset about this."

"Of course, the people who might be upset weren't there," Steve says.

"Well, they had their chance," Kati pipes in.

"Where do we go from here?" Elly asks.

"Let's see what Terry Roof's group comes up with," Ed Potts says, and we move into the agenda. The retrofit of the church continues, the retrofit chair reports. Drilling has begun on the upper roof of the church. The scaffolding is in place to plaster the interior. "We won't be in for Christmas," he says. "But it'll be very soon after that."

The Stewardship Committee is planning a kickoff "Harvest Dinner" of chicken piccate and rice, Betty Bickel says. It's pledge time again. This year we planned a budget with a $17,835 deficit. Next year, the deficit could run well over $30,000. Next year, we'll need to hire a part-time program coordinator to help Mark, and we plan to take over the buildings in which the Montessori school is housed for our burgeoning Sunday school, thus losing the Montessori rent. The Church relies on voluntary giving, and it's plenty scary. This year at Trinity we're dependent on one hundred and eighty "pledging units," persons or families, who pledged a total of one hundred and fifty thousand dollars. (We made an additional sixty-seven thousand dollars from the collection plates on Sundays, special donations, interest income, and offerings at special services.) One false move, one risk taken, and a pledge flies out the door.

Parish Life and Growth reports that we will have our traditional Bring Your Leftovers Potluck on the Sunday after Thanksgiving.

"Salmonella Sunday," Mark says. "Come one, come all."

I'M EDITING THE newsletter for November, trying to meet a deadline for mailing on Friday. The phone rings and I figure it's one or more members of the edit team.

"Yeah," I say picking up.

"Nora, it's Kit."

"Well, hi. Why are you calling me at this expensive hour?"

"Something's not right."

A thin blade runs down my spine. "What do you mean?"

"I just can't pee. The catheter isn't working. And I'm having pain. They want to ream me out on Thursday, and they want to do a biopsy."

"A biopsy?"

"Yeah."

"But the CAT scan was clear."

"I know, Dr. Ortolano says it's a good thing to do while they're in there."

"Do you want me to come?"

"No. Pray for me."

When we hang up, I go outside and sit down.

To pray is to beg, Thomas Jayawardene said in his sermon, and I am begging now. "Protect him," I say, but I find no solace, no helpful calm, nothing. I find nothing.

On Thursday morning, Kit goes into the hospital. We talk briefly and then they take him into surgery. He calls in the evening, groggy and grumpy.

"They won't give me anything to drink yet."

"I love you."

"Yeah, I love you, too, but what I want is something to drink."

In the morning, I call the hospital, but he's sleeping. At ten, because the mailing team has been felled by flu, I go down to the church and sit with Ann Jaqua, another recruit, in the library folding and labeling three hundred and fifty newsletters. At ten-thirty I call the machine at home. Kit has left a message to call him.

I look at Mark's office. The door is open. I don't know where he is.

"I'm going to call New Mexico from Mark's phone," I say to Ann.

"Since the church owes you about fifty thousand dollars in back pay," she replies, "I think it's okay."

I go in and call. Kit answers and his voice is very soft.

"It's recurred."

"Tell me."

"They found some cells."

"What does that mean?"

"I don't know. They have me scheduled for radiation in November."

"Why not chemo?"

"They say it's too soon after the last round. I'm going home now. Call me this afternoon."

I hang up and go back into the library and sit down. Ann is sitting across the table watching me.

"It's recurred," I say.

"Go home," she says.

"No," I say, "I won't know what to do with myself." I start folding, labeling; the names on the labels pass through my hands. In a few minutes, I notice that Ann isn't in the room.

Mark strides through the door at a fast clip followed by Ann; he walks over to my chair and puts his hand on my shoulder.

I grab him around the waist and lean my head against his jacket like a child. I hold on as tight as I can.

"Please," I say into his pocket.

In a little while, he helps me up and walks me out the library door and then out the church door. I hold on to his arm as he walks down the sidewalk to the car. As we walk, I notice that the cosmos need to be deadheaded. I say, "They start radiation. What does it mean, radiation. Why not chemo? I think I'll call Ben Hitz. Who was Lois's doctor here?"

"That's a good idea," Mark says opening my car door. "Do you want me to go back in and get Ben's phone number?"

"No," I say, "I've got it at home."

I get in. I'm still holding on to his arm. I can't figure out how to close the door and hold on to his arm at the same time.

He takes the hand that's holding his arm and places it carefully on the steering wheel, then closes the door. He leans against the window frame.

"Can you drive?"

"Yes."

"Are you sure?"

"Yes."

"I'm sorry."

"Yes," I say.

That evening, Kit and I spend an hour on the phone. I'm in full journalist mode, suggesting "that place in Marin County that was on Bill Moyers," and "Lois's doctor," and the kitchen sink.

"I just don't know what it means," he keeps saying.

IN MY BOX at church on Sunday are two missives: one from the chair of the Parish Life and Growth Council, complaining that she hadn't been able to proof the newsletter because she and the designer had their wires crossed over where and when the proofs were to be delivered to the church. The second is from a woman who once volunteered in the Kitchen. It reads: "To the vestry: The incident referred to in the attached report was extremely upsetting and frightening to me. I was all alone in the building, volunteering in the office.

"I am convinced now more than ever that the Community Kitchen should not be permanently returned to Trinity. Our parishioners, staff, visitors, and the Montessori School children should not be subjected to incidents such as I experienced today.

"The responsibility of feeding the homeless belongs to the *entire* community of Santa Barbara, not just Trinity Episcopal Church. I believe in 'Outreach' but I feel the entire congregation should have input into how and where we 'reach out.' I suggest a vote at the Annual Meeting. This is only fair."

The report is attached: "A very drunk man came to the office window demanding a sack lunch. I explained lunches were now provided by Catholic Charities. The person would not leave. Became verbally abusive, banged on the window when I drew the blinds. Leaned on door buzzer, banged on door—went to all entries trying to get in. Made very frightening threats . . . I was *alone* in the building."

Under "Action Taken" is written, "Police called and arrived within ten minutes of the call. They took the offender away in a patrol car."

I read both notes and then lean against the counter. The vestry will have to take up the issue of the Kitchen's return; I can see it coming. It isn't fair not to. What will I do if the Kitchen doesn't return to Trinity, I think, and what will Trinity do? How will we learn what we need to see?

ON ALL HALLOWS Eve a friend forwards by e-mail a litany from a pastoral minister in Ohio:

> *Lord of Light and Darkness, the days grow short and our*
> *spirits flag, and in the gathering gloom all fears of mortal*
> *humans rear their ugly heads.*
> *From the ghosts of failures that continue to haunt us,*
> *deliver us, O Lord.*
> *From the goblins of people who hurt our pride and our*
> *feelings,*
> *deliver us, O Lord.*
> *. . . From the masks we wear to hide our pain,*
> *deliver us, O Lord.*

We ring the labyrinth with votives and walk in the near dark. The air feels thin, the dead close by. The flames are reflected and multiplied in the window glass. I step into and out of the shadows of the people walking with me. Lois walks in front of me, pencils in her pocket.

"All Hallows Eve is a time for contemplation of the horrors of death—or just plain death—and especially my own death," says a friend. As I walk, I remember my friend Ben's arms as thin as sticks, his yellow-gray skin, the hand that twitched. Lois's distended belly, pieces of Ben's bones. One of the readings for tonight is from Ezekiel, the prophet who mutters of the "dry bones" and the "lost hope" of the house of Israel.

One day while Ben was dying, Mark Grotke and I walked around the corner to get a burger.

"Do you think there's an afterlife?" Mark said, as we crossed State Street.

"I do, but I can't figure out what it is," I said. "I know that the soul goes back to something."

"Sometimes I think that it's okay if there's not an afterlife," Mark said. "You get so tired, maybe it's okay just to lie down."

"In the ground."

"In the ground."

Tonight, when we finish walking the labyrinth, we blow out the candles one by one.

We planned a short base community because we all want to go home and see the kids in their Halloween costumes. Mark Benson reads from "Little Gidding," from T. S. Eliot's *Four Quartets*:

> *The only hope, or else despair,*
> *Lies in the choice of pyre or pyre—*
> *To be redeemed from fire by fire.*
>
> *Who then devised the torment? Love.*
> *Love is the unfamiliar Name*
> *Behind the hands that wove*
> *The intolerable shirt of flame*
> *Which human power cannot remove.*
>
> *We only live, only suspire*
> *Consumed by either fire or fire.*

Earlier this week I asked a friend of mine who is a therapist how to stop projecting my own fears and weakness onto others—that is, how to love—and she replied, "You must enlarge your capacity to suffer."

Tonight I think, That's the fire.

On All Saints Sunday Mark Asman slowly reads the names of everyone who has died in the parish this year: "Evelyn Bourbon, Eloise Lannon, Mildred Hunt, Aurora Vincent, Marion Whelpley, Merith Cecily Brothers, Elizabeth McConell, Rebecca Forsyth, Lois Hitz . . ." All Hallows Eve and All Saints' Day are celebrated back to back in the church, the night of the dead and the day when all are joined together in St. Paul's "great cloud of witnesses."

In Ben's bedroom two years ago, I saw death's destructive powers. And I saw or felt something else as I sat there, day after day, watching Ben breathe on the bed. One day in the early part of his dying, he said, "I like the silence. It has majesty." In that majestic silence, I felt the thing that was waiting for Ben. It filled the room with its power, its sweetness, its light. Day after day, it grew larger. Its air was like pure oxygen and its power great enough to create a universe. And yet it was so gentle, so respectful of Ben, it only waited for him, a hand held out.

In the early afternoon, I visit Barbara Kelly, who used to attend the Thursday Eucharist. She's been in and out of the hospital all year. Now she's close to death, the pain barely covered by morphine.

"Are all of you her family?" a nurse asks. "There are so many of you."

Later, I drive up to the monastery to spend a few hours with a friend and go to vespers. She and I are lounging outside in the sun on deck chairs like ship's passengers, reading, when Robert opens the door, a tray of tea and cookies in his hand.

"Excuse me ladies," he says quietly. "But I believe we've hit an iceberg."

At five-thirty, the monks chant:

> *O gracious Light,*
> *pure brightness of the ever living Father in heaven,*
> *O Jesus Christ, holy and blessed,*
> *now as we come to the setting of the sun*
> *and our eyes behold the vesper light*
> *we sing your praises, O God: Father, Son and Holy Spirit.*

When they are finished, the monks pad out, one by one. I close my eyes. In the distance, through the thick chapel walls, I can hear their voices, as they prepare to serve supper. I can't make out the words but I can hear the deep bass bell of Brother Allan followed by the lilt of William's tenor, and Robert's light laugh. The sounds of their voices wash my ears, are miracle enough.

That night, I dream I am serving communion with George Barrett. The wafers are in what my mother used to call a "portable butler," a brass pan with a long handle and a hinged cover. At cocktail parties, I used to walk around with our "butler" and dump ashtrays into it. In the dream, the wafers are strewn amid ashes, cigarette butts, and bits of paper. George and I rescue the wafers with a slotted spoon and serve them to the assembled people, many of whom are from Trinity. We say together, "The Body of Christ, the Bread of Heaven." It's salvage work, I think when I wake up in the morning, a consecration.

Cynthia rides down on the train for a visit and comes to church with me for the first time. Afterward she says to Ann Jaqua, "I find it all hard to believe," and sweeps her hand toward the altar and the cross.

"So do I," Ann replies. "That's why I end up here week after week."

In the Kitchen, we feed two hundred people in two and a half hours. Ann and I make two and a half pots of white beans, onions, potatoes, carrots, celery, and what might be jicama, and from then on we just keep throwing chopped vegetables into a pot of water and praying for it to boil. Outside in the dining room, Christina carries a bowl of water and a Handi Wipe, wiping down tables. She looks like a nurse ministering at the front. Arriving at one table she announces, "It looks like there was an all-night poker game here."

The men reply, "The guys before us were slobs."

I walk into the kitchen at one point, or rather run in, and take in this scene: four volunteers furiously chopping onions, potatoes, cabbage, and broccoli. Dodie at the sink, surrounded by muddy spinach. A volunteer named Ellen Lee up to her aristocratic elbows in grapefruit rind; a whole table covered with plastic bags, vegetable peelings, fruit juice, opened cans, bags of dried beans, and a bin of rotting zucchini.

Ingrid, a Lutheran ten years my senior, tells me to move out of the way so she can get the bread out of the oven.

"You could say 'please,'" I say.

"The alternative is to slap your butt," she replies.

ON FRIDAY EVENING, November 17, Vincent and I are watching a movie on TV when the phone rings. I answer in the kitchen, standing up at the counter. It's Kit. He sounds very far away, his voice fogged.

"I went to see the radiologist today and he told me he figured I knew I had zero percent chance of recovery," Kit says. "I told him no, I didn't know that. He said there was a tumor in my urethra and one in a lymph node. That meant the cancer was spreading. It would go up my torso. He said I have months to a year."

"Kit," I say.

"I drove home slowly, it was a very strange drive home. They hadn't given me any warning. Rande wasn't with me. I drank two beers, had some Valium.

"I told him I was afraid of dying in pain in a hospital. He said he had a lot of drugs that would help me and, 'No one wants to die in a hospital. We'll do what we can.' He said, 'We don't know each other now but we will know each other.'"

"Kit," I say. "Let me come."

"You're coming right after Christmas," he says.

"But I could come now," I reply.

"Baby sister," he says. "Let's talk in the morning."

I realize that Vincent is standing right behind me. When I hang up, he folds me into his arms.

In the morning, Kit's voice is sweet. He says, "Don't know what to do, don't know what to do."

I call Lois's doctor, the head of a cancer foundation here. I tell him what the radiologist said to Kit.

"That is not something anyone should say," he replies, and agrees to read Kit's medical reports. Kit gives permission and his doctors fax them over.

"I can't quite figure this out," the doctor says. "But there is never a zero percent."

Kit and I are talking every day now. I ask him if I can pay for flying him to one of the cancer centers, in Houston or Los Angeles.

"I don't think so," he says. "I have an image of what those places are like. There's a room with the white rats in one corner and me in the other."

In a few days, his voice is stronger, almost serene.

"I figure there is always a point-five-percent chance,"

he says. "That's what I told the radiologist when I saw him yesterday."

In another few days he says he's decided to go on a macrobiotic diet. I send Rande two cookbooks.

"Maybe I shouldn't have done the chemo," he says.

"How is your pain?"

"It's a bit better. I think the radiation actually helps. But it makes me so tired."

On Thanksgiving, I call him, but his phone is out of order. We can only barely hear each other.

I yell, "I love you," through the static. "Happy Thanksgiving."

"I love you," comes his muffled reply.

ANNE HOWARD MAKES the sign of the cross at the end of the Eucharist, at the end of Ordinary Time.

"May you walk with God," she says.

And we reply, "In the sharp pain of growing."

"In the midst of confusion."

"In the bright light of knowing."

"May you live in God."

"In God's constant compassion."

"In God's infinite wisdom."

"In God's passion for peace."

"May you walk with God."

"And live in God."

"And remain with God."

"This night, and forever. Amen."

THE LIGHT FADES into winter. Kit calls and says he's eating macrobiotic and meditating twice a day. When meditating, he had a "vision" in which he "pissed out all the bad stuff in lumps." He sounds strong and sane. "See you right after Christmas," we say to each other.

I walk the labyrinth after many people have walked it all day long. Even as I enter, I can feel all those prayers as if they've built up the ground, prepared the way. I'm flooded by memories: the light fur of the palomino horse I had as a child; my father's hand on my head; my mother bringing me a low tray filled with white flour, for snow, and tiny figures—animals, men, women, and children—with which to build a village scene, a story. Kit on crutches when he was fourteen, having broken his leg skiing, playing tag with me among red poppies. Faith rises up out of ordinary days; the stone in my pocket is made sacred by the hands of the person who gave it to me. I ask God a simple question: How will I live now, with my brother so ill, what can I do? As I walk one of the great outer rings, I feel the purest peace. And the answer comes, this thinnest of threads: everything is contained in my love, even this.

O N N I C H O L A S F E R R A R 's feast day, I meet Ann Jaqua for lunch outside at Brigitte's Café, two blocks down the street from Trinity. We refer to it as "our club." We're planning a project with two artists who've just joined Trinity and it's meeting with resistance from the liturgy committee.

I order Brigitte's special, a half-sandwich and a salad, but they bring me a whole sandwich.

"Sometimes I just can't stand church life," I say to Ann, biting into a sandwich half.

"You have two options," she replies. "Live with it or start a new one."

While we're talking, a crazy man with dreadlocks and a bare chest saunters by. He used to come to the Kitchen when it was housed at Trinity.

When we are finished, I stand up, the half-sandwich still on my plate.

"I don't know what to do with this," I say to Ann. "I'm going to see my therapist and she doesn't have a refrigerator."

The crazy man walks back down the street. He stops near the table, looks at me.

"You gonna eat that?"

"No," I say, and hand it to him. It's a smooth motion without effort or hesitation.

Ann grins. She says, "Nothing is lost."

ACKNOWLEDGMENTS

When Anne Howard returned from Norway in 1995, she reported that on many headstones is the single word *takk*, thanks.

Thanks to and for

Cynthia Gorney and Anne Howard, Ann Jaqua and Mark Asman

My editor at Knopf, Jane Garrett

My agent at Sterling Lord Literistic, Flip Brophy

Ellen Meloy, Jodie Ireland, Anne Makepeace, and Peter Behrens

David, Julie, Sean, and Robert Gallagher and Rande Brown

Elizabeth Corrigan, George Barrett, Dodie Little, Eleanor Cuthbertson, and Ben Hitz

The Thursday Night Base Community: Katrina, Mark Benson, Elizabeth, Robin, Mandy, Richard, Joe, Nancy, Marjorie, David, Danuta, and Lois

The Community Kitchen: Faustino, Alan, Little Alex, Peter, Greg, Larry, and Juli

Trinity's vestry: Betty Bickel, Leslie Campbell, Al Christ, Stephen Gibson, Michael Harris, Mandy McCoy, Ed Potts, Terry Roof, Colleen Sterne, and Nancy Tustian

Acknowledgments

The wider Church: Christina Fernandez, Dawn George, Scott Richardson, Robert Hagler, Mark Grotke, Jim and Corrie Lassen-Willems, Larry Donoghue, Bob Mosher, and Edmond Browning

At Patagonia: Malinda and Yvon Chouinard, Joanne Dornan, John Dutton, Betsy Haygood, Kim Myers, and Elissa Pfost

Thanks to and for Vincent, fierce true love.

NOTES

Advent

4   "a desacralized earth": Jeremy Rifkin, speech at Patagonia, Inc., Ventura, Calif., January 1992.

John Berger, "The Production of the World," *The Sense of Sight* (New York: Pantheon, 1985), 278–79.

5   "intimate promise" and "Mary's appalled assent": Janet Morley, *All Desires Known* (Harrisburg, Penn.: Morehouse Publishing, 1992), 26.

W. H. Auden, "Musée des Beaux Arts," *The Modern Poets* (New York: McGraw-Hill, 1970), 20.

6   "radical theology": Richard Giles, *Repitching the Tent* (Norwich, England: Canterbury Press, 1997), 9.

"ordered . . . many of his curates could not read": Owen Chadwick, *The Reformation* (London: Penguin Books, 1990), 103.

7   "attended Mass three times a day": ibid., 23.

"at once delicate and austere": ibid., 119.

8   "membership . . . declined 15 percent": The 1985 Report of the Committee on the State of the Church, National Episcopal Church.

10   "O unknown God . . .": Morley, *All Desires Known*, 5.

"Religion is nothing . . .": as quoted in William James, *Varieties of Religious Experience* (New York: The Modern Library, 1936), 454.

12   "I wake to sleep, . . .": Theodore Roethke, "The Waking," *The Collected Poems of Theodore Roethke* (New York: Doubleday, 1966), 104.

13   "Be like the fox. . . . Practice resurrection": Wendell Berry, "Manifesto: The Mad Farmer Liberation Front," *Collected Poems* (New York: North Point Press/Farrar, Straus and Giroux, 1984), 151.

15   "quietly invisible, mystical interconnectedness": Scott Peck, back of book jacket for *Congregation* by Gary Dorsey (New York: Viking, 1995).

18   "It was a practice in which ordinary": Esther de Waal, "The Extraordinary in the Ordinary," *Weavings* (May/June 1987), 8.

"The blessing of God": Vienna Cobb Anderson, *Prayers of Our Hearts in Word and Action* (New York: Crossroad, 1991), 208.

Notes

26 "A priest is essentially": Urban Holmes, "The Priest," *Ministry and Imagination* (New York: Seabury Press, 1976), 221.

27 de Waal, "The Extraordinary in the Ordinary," 15.

Christmas

28 "The world is God's body": Grace Jantzen, *God's World, God's Body* (Philadelphia: Westminster Press, 1984).

33 "that we should duly use them": Thirty-nine Articles, Article XXV, The Book of Common Prayer.
"the blessed mutter of the Mass": John Moorman, *The Anglican Spiritual Tradition* (Springfield, Ill.: Templegate Publishers, 1983), 20.

46 *"contemptus mundi"*: Thomas Merton, *Conjectures of a Guilty Bystander* (New York: Doubleday, 1966), 50–51.

57 "what the world has done to them": Alice Neel, notes from "Kinships: Alice Neel Looks at the Family," an exhibit of her portraits at the Art Museum, University of California at Santa Barbara, 1997.

Epiphany

64 "to be a 'living sacrifice' ": The Book of Common Prayer, Rite II, Eucharist Prayer D, 375.

67 "Once baptized . . . pursuit of private ends": Philip Turner, "Limited Engagements," *Men and Women, Sexual Ethics in Turbulent Times* (Cambridge, Mass.: Cowley Publications, 1989), 82.

70 "It was the first time . . .": George Orwell, *Homage to Catalonia* (Boston: Beacon Press, 1967), 54–55.

72 "To free the patient from the slavery of impersonal behavior": W. H. Auden, "Greatness Finding Itself," in a review of Erik Erikson's biography of Martin Luther, *Forewords and Afterwords* (New York: Random House, 1973), 79.

73 "the despised layers of social hierarchy": Simone Weil, letter to Georges Bernanos, in *Escrits historiques et politiques* (Paris: Gallimard, 1960), 220–24.

77 "an impulse of an essentially and manifestly different order . . . the greatest of all ills": Simone Weil, "Spiritual Autobiography," *Waiting for God* (New York: Harper and Row, 1951), 63.

Lent

81 "what it meant to be Jesus": Frederick Buechner, *Whistling in the Dark* (San Francisco: HarperSanFrancisco, 1988), 82.

82 "Jesus, remember me": Taize, volume 1, Les Presses de Taize, France, 1981. In the US: GIA Publications, Inc., 7407 So. Mason Ave., Chicago, Illinois. 60638.

"ashes to fire": Richard Pervo, "Lent," Proclamation 5, Series C, Interpreting the Lessons of the Church Year (Minneapolis: Fortress Press, 1994), 13.

85 "live within the truth": Václav Havel, "The Power of the Powerless," *Living in Truth* (London: Faber and Faber, 1989), 55.

86 "Until the sixties": Mary S. Donovan, *Women Priests in the Episcopal Church* (Cincinnati: Forward Movement, 1988), 5.
"Not until 1970": ibid., 6.

91 "physical sexual expression is appropriate . . . deviates and departs from the biblical norm": in a letter, "Response to the Opinion of the Court for the Trial of a Bishop," signed by Bishop Schofield (and nine other bishops), May 1996.

106 "Abbot Lot . . . changed into fire": Desert Fathers LXXII, as quoted in Esther de Waal, *Seeking God: The Way of St. Benedict* (Collegeville, Minnesota: Liturgical Press, 1984), 37.

Holy Week

107 "the set pieces . . . without their getting killed": Annie Dillard, *Holy the Firm* (New York: Harper and Row, 1977), 59.

108 "For a people to do their liturgy . . . and the wine": Gabe Huck, *The Three Days* revised edition (Chicago: Liturgy Training Publications, 1992), 57.

111 "house churches": Karen Torjesen, *When Women Were Priests* (San Francisco: HarperSanFrancisco, 1993), 6.
"informal, often countercultural . . . leadership roles": ibid., 11.
"an alternative family": ibid., 126.
"teaching, disciplining . . . administrating": ibid., 82.

118 "I believed . . . be in trouble": Daniel Berrigan in *The Geography of Faith*, by Robert Coles and Daniel Berrigan (Boston: Beacon Press, 1971), 81.

121 "nuisances and nobodies" and "an open commensality": John Dominic Crossan, *Jesus: A Revolutionary Biography* (New York: HarperCollins, 1994), 54, 66.

122 "with sharp social boundaries . . . Jew and Gentile": Marcus Borg, *Meeting Jesus Again for the First Time* (San Francisco: HarperSanFrancisco, 1994), 51, 52.

125 "everything upside down . . . did not fall down": Frank Rogers, Jr., sermon at the School of Theology at Claremont, California, 1995.
"I know Jesus drinks himself . . .": Anne Lamott, *San Francisco Chronicle*, April 25, 1994.

129 "It is like the Pietà": David Richo, "The Void," retreat at Trinity Episcopal Church, Santa Barbara, May 10, 1997.

Eastertide

136 "A Note on Story . . . into a new story": James Hillman, *Loose Ends* (Dallas: Spring Publications, 1975), 2.

137 "Her cookin's lousy . . . it's home": Tom Lehrer, "I Wanna Go Back to Dixie," *Too Many Songs by Tom Lehrer* (New York: Pantheon, 1981), 26.

"watchmen taking shifts": Paul Elie, "Saint Thomas, Apostle," *A Tremor of Bliss*, Paul Elie, editor (New York: Riverhead Books, 1995), 224.

Pentecost

160 "The labyrinth is a . . . tool . . .": "Pilgrimage of the Soul": interview with Lauren Artress by Jerry Snider in *Magical Blend* (November 1993–January 1994), 63.

"Today, we've lost touch . . .": Interview with Lauren Artress in *Common Boundary* (March/April 1992), 43–44.

163 "Celtic monks . . . guests of the world": Esther de Waal, *Every Earthly Blessing* (Ann Arbor, Mich.: Servant Publications, 1991), 53–54.

"Pilgrims are persons in motion . . .": Richard Neibuhr, "Pilgrims and Pioneers," *Parabola* (Fall 1984), 7–10.

175 "Forsaken, almost human": Leonard Cohen, "Suzanne," Project Seven Music, 1966.

177 "Itinerarium Salisburgense": J. G. Davies, *Pilgrimage Yesterday and Today* (London: SCM Press, 1988), 20.

"In 1139, it took . . . one trip to the Holy Land": Alan Kendall, *Medieval Pilgrims* (London: Wayland Publishers, 1970), 45.

"All pilgrimages . . . no good in them": Davies, *Pilgrimage Yesterday and Today*, 98.

186 "A corrupt version . . . that is not morality": James Holloway, interview on "Newsnight," September 1997.

187 "Church Court to Try Bishop . . . a non-celibate homosexual": Larry Stammer, *Los Angeles Times*, August 19, 1995.

"There is not now . . . of the Roman Catholic Church": W. Taylor Stevenson, "Lex Orandi–Lex Credendi," *The Study of Anglicanism*, Stephen Sykes and John Booty, editors (Minneapolis: SPCK/Fortress Press, 1988), 174.

188 "The question is . . . order and unity": Gustav Niebuhr, *New York Times*, August 28, 1995.

199 "Come now, disturbing . . . release resurrection in the world": Janet Morley, *All Desires Known* (Harrisburg, Penn.: Morehouse Publishing, 1992), 55.

Notes

Ordinary Time

202 "keeping a rendezvous" and "the whole of themselves . . . are the same thing": John Berger, "The Soul and the Operator," *Keeping a Rendezvous* (New York: Vintage, 1992), 228.

203 "We thank you God for . . . which is Yes": e.e. cummings, "#95," *100 Selected Poems* (New York: Grove Press, 1954), 114.

209 "No sense of joy . . . emotions at all": C. S. Lewis, *A Grief Observed* (New York: Bantam Books, 1961), 86.

214 "My limbs . . . Beloved, tell me!": as quoted in Carol Lee Flinders, *Enduring Grace* (San Francisco: HarperSanFrancisco, 1993), 62.

215 "God our lover . . . through Jesus Christ, Amen": Janet Morley, *All Desires Known* (Harrisburg, Penn.: Morehouse Publishing, 1992), 20.

226 "Lord of Light and Darkness . . . deliver us, O Lord": Halloween prayer, Michalene Murphy, St. Patrick Church, Kent, Ohio, November 1, 1996.

227 "The only hope . . . Consumed by either fire or fire": T. S. Eliot, "Little Gidding," *The Four Quartets* (New York: Harcourt Brace Jovanovich, 1971), 57.

232 "May you walk with God . . . This night, and forever. Amen": Benediction, from A Eucharist on the Feast Day of St. Mary Magdalene, All Saints Church, Pasadena, Calif., July 22, 1994.